1/99   1,50

NUCLEAR ENCHANTMENT

NUCLEAR ENCHANTMENT

Photographs by Patrick Nagatani

Essay by Eugenia Parry Janis

University of New Mexico Press  **Albuquerque**

Library of Congress Cataloging in Publication Data

Nagatani, Patrick, 1945–
    Nuclear enchantment / Patrick Nagatani ; essay by Eugenia Parry Janis.—1st ed.
        p.   cm.
    ISBN 0-8263-1271-3.—ISBN 0-8263-1272-1 (pbk.)
    1. Photography, Documentary—New Mexico.   2. Nuclear industry—New Mexico—
Pictorial works.   I. Janis, Eugenia Parry.   II. Title.
    TR820.5.N333   1991
    779′.9978—dc20
    91-3523
        CIP

To my parents—P.N.

CONTENTS

A HOT IRON BALL
HE CAN NEITHER
SWALLOW NOR SPIT OUT

Patrick Nagatani, Nuclear Fear, and the Uses of Enchantment

Eugenia Parry Janis

WHAT ARE YOU DOING? WHAT ARE YOU SAYING?

His slender body is rigid as a rail. His face, under the baseball cap turned backwards, is a No mask; but the eyes flash like comets, and the mind is lightning. He is chronically intense, almost manic as he plots in exquisite detail the ideas for his photographs. The poetics of color chemistries are therapeutic: for six years he traveled to New York, Boston, San Diego, and to Offenbach in Germany to use Polaroid's 20-×-24-inch camera. Its technologies inspired him to construct large, high-strung, operatic fabrications of his subject matter which prick the conscience and provoke laughter. There was no darkroom work; Polaroid color guaranteed it. To photograph he simply opened the aperture on a fully conceived tableau vivant. The exposure was little more than a final gesture, a punctuation mark that completed a complex sentence. Recently, his art of profound preconception has changed its course, but then, so has his sense of humor.

"Atomic Cafe," 1983, Nagatani/Tracey.

From 1983 Patrick Nagatani's photographic working methods, especially in collaboration with the painter Andrée Tracey, far surpassed the theatrics of what has been called photography's directoral mode. The events they recorded were chaotic prosceniums of dark humor that walked the tightrope between funhouse terror and sitcom buffoonery. A moralizing invective always lurked in the work, but most people were too tickled by the luscious hues and the hilarity to notice it, such were Nagatani's subversive, satirical skills. Now working without Tracey, he remains dedicated to lampooning but also feels liberated from her love of making light of an idea; he feels freer to explore and realign the darker premonitions of his observations.

In this new phase he has begun to reclaim and reexamine many kinds of expertise, not the least of these being his early training as a designer. If designers' methods have always influenced the way he conceives of photographs, he employs the old tools now with greater self-scrutiny. No longer relying on Tracey's painting, he finds other ways to dress his scenes. He has begun to intensify a boyhood obsession with building scale models by putting himself on the mailing list of "The Squadron," a hobby store in Carrollton, Texas, which supplies decals and models of every miniature in the world that pertains to modern military history.

In recent years Nagatani has built from kits over one hundred of these models. Most are aircraft involved with nuclear weapons. They include a B-29 like the *Enola Gay,* which dropped the atomic bomb on Hiroshima; a Nike-Hercules missile, the first ground-to-air anti-aircraft weapon designed to carry a nuclear warhead; a B-36 Strategic Air Command bomber; two F-111D Aardvarks, long-range fighter jets of the type that make more than 1,800 annual subsonic sorties from Cannon Air Force base at Clovis, New Mexico, their only center of operations in North America; an F-117, the virtually invisible Stealth fighter whose titanium base is meant to evade radar detection; an A7-D used by the Air National Guard out of New Mexico's Kirtland Air Force base; two F-16 Falcon fighter planes, numbers 5 and 6 from the Air Force Thunderbird Performance Team; an F-15 Eagle; a C-130 cargo plane, and at least two hundred ground-to-air missiles and bombs. Although such plastic designs often appeared in earlier fabrications, Nagatani uses them now to create the entire setting for a shot. On the A-7D (Plate 16), which took an entire summer to complete, he illusionistically hand-painted all of the rivets, nuts, and bolts. He searched hobby shops around the country for the proper New Mexico Air National Guard decal markings for the plane, finally finding them in Los Angeles.

Plate 16

Nagatani's love of fanciful precision in toys led him years ago to Hollywood where for a while he painted sets, but more significantly, fell in love with the fanatical attention to detail, arranged for the camera eye alone, demanded by the cinematic geniuses of special effects. Although he has given up sharing the authorship of his photographs with a single partner, his new work upholds Hollywood's special effects tradition, by continuing to need the well-calibrated involvement of numerous technical and inspirational contributors at every stage.

Building models may require meditative isolation, but as a photographic fabricator Nagatani hardly ever works alone. This fact distinguishes his art and places him in a category clearly outside of the traditional solitude of the modernist. Since his vision for the new work actually exaggerates the complexity of the pictorial staging fundamental to his imagination, he continues to invite others to aid him and join the fun. Actually, their participation reinforces the intensity of the layered meanings he strives for. It is not surprising at the outset of the project to see Nagatani working closely with a poet who creates dense, verbal equivalents of the photographed subjects and adds to these texts long, arcane annotations of almost talmudic complexity.[1]

Thus, in making his new images the photographer continues to confront all of the problems of teamwork. The ironies he conveys in these pictures are not fixed through his direction, even though he provides their basic conception. The meanings evolve in the course of the staging, through continual dialogues between Nagatani and his technical "experts." Among these are other photographers called in to engineer certain shots, printers who help him "punch up" the colors and fine-tune the different relationships between them, the poet who leads Nagatani to new sites and sources, the student assistants who work as actors or set painters—all on his team become obsessives like himself.[2]

An underlying theme in Nagatani's art has always been the conflict and comedy in collective ideologies. Now he is looking at the boundless faith we have in scientific expertise, and our trust in a peculiar technological ministry, to which we as a nation have given unparalleled freedom. Nagatani's most recent photographic confabulations are dedicated to America's devotion to nuclear power, but more pointedly, the work honors New Mexico, for better or worse, as the mother goddess of the nuclear age. In forty lavish tableaux with color so saturated it seems practically to emit radioactivity, he explores the physical traces of New Mexico's enchantment with the growth of her offspring and throughout the state its effect on the culture there.

Nagatani finds nuclear rapture reflected in many corners, but also he sees that it has suffered changes since the heyday of the first atomic blast at Trinity. He visits a now defunct restaurant in Grants, New Mexico, called The Uranium Cafe; he shoots a bar in Alamogordo called Rocket Lounge (Plate 28); he creates a scene of monuments commemorating notable missiles which decorate the lawns outside Alamogordo's Chamber of Commerce to show that these spindly icons, silhouetted against a sky of sulphur, mark with dreary ambivalence a diminishing confidence in "up and atom" might (Plate 27).

In a similar spirit of dismay Nagatani fills his camera frame with dune-like encrustations of uranium tailings left by the Anaconda Minerals Corporation at the Laguna Pueblo Reservation (Plate 6); or those the Homestake Mining Company deposited near Mount Taylor, Milan, and Grants (Plate 5); or the United Nuclear

Plate 28

Plate 6

Corporation uranium mill's tailings dump in the area of Church Rock. In this photo he applies the healing imprimatur of Hiroshige's golden eagle, symbol of power and authority but also of recovery (Plate 8).[3] He discovers a desolate horizon of tailings alongside Navajo tract homes at Shiprock and paints the sky cadmium red. To suggest the loss of beautiful Indian land he superimposes on this wasteland a foldout image, like a fantastic postcard, of the formerly blue skies and sacred clay of "Bida Hi" (Plate 10). With Japanese motifs he invents other poetic equations in order to tell the story. One, in the manner of a supremely peaceful Japanese New Year's card showing gently falling snow, gives a perverse twist to his rendition of a landscape of radioactive waste, dumped since the 1940s, which today contaminates Mortandad Canyon southeast of Los Alamos and seems headed underground toward Cochiti Lake (Plate 11). Or he considers the "mismatch of strengths between radioactivity and genetic material,"[4] as he engulfs in green phosphorescence a supine patient undergoing radiation treatment for cancer (Plate 33).

Plate 8

For this series entitled *Nuclear Enchantment* Nagatani assumes the role of a mock high priest who contrives to suggest, through an elaborate pictorial miserere, a gradual numbing of awareness to what nuclear power means, not only in the conduct of daily life in New Mexico but, by implicaton, everywhere in the modern world. In the process he has also reawakened another of his skills, the systematic exploitation of which is relatively new to him, especially in the extreme measures he has taken to use it. He has become a calculating gumshoe.

Plate 10

Nagatani likes to think that if he weren't an artist he would have been a historian. But this wishful thinking doesn't begin to describe the way he marshals his curiosity these days. In his research into nuclear affairs he pursues and collects public information with maniacal single-mindedness. Exquisitely patient, and blessed with resilient good cheer more typical of a well-schooled student of Zen than an artist or detective, for the past few years he has undertaken a personal quest, not only to survey and monitor New Mexico's public lands, but to learn what kinds of stories are being told about the relationship between dubiously progressive scientific and military nuclear activities and our society's gradual desecration of the earth. This change in orientation has taken Nagatani from his hermetically sealed photographic theaters quite literally into the field to do

Plate 11

5

reconnaissance work. There he photographs less than he attempts to find out what is going on, and who is doing what.

He admits that his investigations are merely those of an interested private citizen; but actually, they have more to do with the kinds of artistic choices that interest him. His reverence for New Mexico's ethereal landscape and for the Native American cultures is profound. He confesses he has never experienced anything like the beauty of New Mexico anywhere. He wants to remain in this place. But his choice to do so is sharpened by a set of local conditions which intensify his awareness of threatening nuclear dangers worldwide. Thus, as an artist of unbounded curiosity and persistence, he is in a situation greatly to his liking: he has discovered a wonderful place to live, but better yet, a place worth investigating.

Patrick Nagatani moved to Albuquerque from Los Angeles in 1987. Wherever he goes, his habit is to try and understand the meanings behind the scenery. Soon, he noticed, "people began telling me things."[5] And he began to gather information about the nuclear industry in a region which "contains the most extensive nuclear weapons research, management, training, and testing facilities and organization in the United States."[6] Direct evidence for this hit him instantly. He describes his first observations:

Plate 22

In Chicago or Los Angeles or wherever I've lived, I've never seen the amount of military aircraft that I see out here. You know, I'm driving down Interstate 40 to go to see relatives in Texas and suddenly, maybe only two hundred feet above I-40, coming right over my head—I recognize all these planes—is an F-111D Aardvark attack bomber from Clovis, from Cannon. This is the only place in the country where you see these things because it's the only base in North America, here in New Mexico, that we have them. They're all aimed at Central America for rapid deployment. They're based in Cannon, but they're out for training flights. They go to Colorado, presumably for mock bombing runs; so they fly right over the highway going out to Colorado. This is another issue in the state, of the noise of low-flying aircraft and the possibility of them crashing. I can almost recognize

them by sound now; I know an A-7D flying out of Kirtland or an F-15 Eagle out of Holloman.

Nagatani's earlier work with Tracey in Los Angeles only peripherally touched on issues regarding nuclear testing, the Japanese infatuation with technology, and the fate of the earth. It was the team's great pleasure to portray these themes by cloaking them in the aura of a fairy tale. On their life-sized sets they combined actual players with those made of cardboard; their painted backdrops in funny-paper hues also had an unreal and distancing flatness. Nagatani learned in coming to New Mexico that the nuclear love affair there was wrapped in the aura of a dream without his having to do much to create the effect. Nearly every descriptive account of nuclear research or report of nuclear testing that he read seemed to drift into hallucinative fancy.

The photographer consumes Pulitzer Prize–winning accounts of the construction of the atomic bomb because he loves the glorious dramas of their countdowns, their marvelous accuracy of detail, but the closer the documentation comes to reconstructing the truth, moment by moment, the more it resembles the special effects the artist had loved so much in Hollywood.

At 5:29:35 A.M. on July 16, 1945, for example, a group of scientists from Los Alamos, having jerry-rigged a "gadget" made of some plugs containing plutonium, polonium alphas, and uranium on top of a one-hundred-foot steel tower in a flat scrub region sixty miles northwest of Alamogordo, set off a test of the first atomic bomb. It is often told that in the first blinding instants of the light of the Trinity blast Robert Oppenheimer, director of the Los Alamos Scientific Laboratory, thought of some apt and beautiful fragments from the Bhagavad-Gita. Trinity has since made them famous:

First nuclear explosion at Trinity Site, White Sands, New Mexico, July 16, 1945. Photograph on display at the Atomic Museum in Albuquerque.

> **If the radiance of a thousand suns**
> **Were to burst at once into the sky**
> **That would be like the splendor**
> **of the Mighty One . . .**
> **I am become Death,**
> **The shatterer of worlds.**

But the statistics of the explosion have their own mantra-like cadences:

The temperature at its center was four times that at the center of the sun; and more than 10,000 times that at the sun's surface. The pressure caving in the ground beneath was over 100 billion atmospheres, the most ever to occur at the earth's surface. The radioactivity emitted was equal to one million times that of the world's total radium supply.[7]

Nagatani commits most of this to memory.

In many accounts that he reads the principal actors in Trinity's fireball theater play their roles as if cast in an animated short subject. The photographer finds obscurity and mystery reigning in narratives of the blast, not only because of the secret nature of the undertaking. Almost everything about early atomic experimentation, like Central Intelligence work, seems to lead its chroniclers to portray an atmosphere of paranoia. Given the virgin territory of the experimentation, most of the scientific decisions were based on partial knowledge, and, to a large extent, on the hunches and feelings of very brilliant men. The site for Trinity, chosen by Oppenheimer, was intended to be as desolate as possible. It lay between the Rio Grande and the Sierra Oscura. Since Spanish times this place had been known as the Jornada del Muerto—the Dead Man's Trail, the Journey of Death. It couldn't have been more appropriate for the romancing historians.

Long before the Spanish presence, a vast area around Trinity belonged to the Anasazi who engraved drawings of fish, birds, mountain lions, cougars, masks, and ripening corn on the stones along a chain of ridges at nearby Three Rivers. These enduring petroglyphs, the drawing of which demonstrates a tender humanism, continue to remind us that centuries before, a region determined as perfect to harbor "death, the shatterer of worlds" had exploded with every evidence of life for people whose weapons hardly surpassed fish hooks and spears. Every new stage of human development thrives by its selective memory. The Los Alamos scientists in the middle 1940s saw only an abandoned stage waiting for a new drama. It was the perfect atmosphere of secrecy, reflected in the stage whispers of Trinity's chroniclers.

Monument marking ground zero at Trinity Site.

Replica of "Fat Man" atomic bomb at Trinity Site (open twice a year, in April and October, for the public).

The drama near Alamogordo had aspects of high jinx too. And Nagatani devours them. The scientists had created the toy of the century. It had no name. They called it "the thing," "the device," "the beast."[8] The general confusion and frailty of the superior human intelligences involved in Trinity emerges in Oppenheimer's recollections of the anxiety before the test where "even a group of scientists is not proof against the errors of suggestion and hysteria." He was not referring to the experimental work with the bomb. Rather, in the hours just before the blast he noted that some of his colleagues stood out in the night sky with binoculars and pondered shooting down some alien object, which turned out to be Venus.[9]

Dr. Edward Teller's precaution to protect himself and the other scientists from the radioactivity during the actual blast perfectly summarizes the cloud of uncertainty and ignorance that shrouded the nuclear community. Installed in the middle of the night at the viewing site of Compania Hill, twenty miles northwest of Ground Zero, he remembered:

We were told to lie down on the sand, turn our faces away from the blast, and bury our heads in our arms. No one complied. We were determined to look the beast in the eye. I wouldn't turn away . . . but having made all those calculations, I thought the blast might be rather bigger than expected. So I put on some suntan lotion.[10]

It is difficult to believe that the destructive implications of the first atomic test were so imperfectly grasped by the scientists themselves, but Nagatani's principal inspiration has been to discover the extent to which the condition has mysteriously remained so.

Present-day myths about nuclear power have lulled most citizens into a state of dreaming. It is no accident that the photographer shows the population around the Alamogordo Chamber of Commerce as faceless automatons carrying attaché cases (Plate 27). But what began to attract him irresistibly in the course of his research was New Mexico's assumption of a "spurious normality,"[11] and an amount of evidence there to suggest that the nuclear fairy tale continues to be perpetuated by an ideology that interweaves scientific truths with zealous

Plate 27

9

misrepresentation and institutional numbness. A fervent belief in the marvelous power of the atom bomb has sunk its adherents into somnambulant and malevolent ignorance, symptoms of the "enervation, dulled senses, enfeebled will, stupor, and paralysis" that only leads to death.[12]

This is the appeal of the myth of nuclear energy to an artist like Nagatani. For him, as for many artists, the issue has become magically symbolic. Now, the mysterious and invisible all-seeing, all-destroying "rays" which had fascinated people for millennia have acquired a concrete manifestation. What is more, their annihilating potential suggests the utopian possibility of totally reorganizing society and life itself. "You destroy me. You are good for me," Marguerite Duras's heroine repeats endlessly in *Hiroshima, Mon Amour.* Through cerebral destruction might come a cerebral rebirth, a complete fulfillment of the promises of the age of Aquarius. Thus, through nuclear power the secret thoughts of many come into the open at last. "We can deny them no longer."[13] From this confidence Nagatani makes his nuclear pictures.

EATING THE BLAME

Patrick Nagatani was born in Chicago on August 19, 1945, thirteen days after the B-29 *Enola Gay* on August 6 at 8:16 A.M. dropped a fission bomb with a yield of twelve and a half kilotons that detonated 1,900 feet above the central section of Hiroshima. His parents are Japanese-Americans, but his father's family lived outside of Hiroshima. Thus Patrick feels keenly marked as a child of the nuclear age, cradled in the gossamer of the mushroom cloud while some of his relatives near Hiroshima struggled to survive in the firey plume of lethal fallout.

If Nagatani has discovered in nuclear enchantment a perfect subject matter for his habit of artistic thinking, he also has found the means to explore something to him more illusory, the contradictory sides of his identity as a Japanese-American. We will examine the way he has pursued the atomic issue and how it touches many facets of his sense of irony. In discussing the imagery in *Nuclear Enchantment* and how playfully it was made, we will arrive at a portrait of the artist's peculiar ingenuity and moral complexity.

Fundamental to Nagatani's penetrating look at New Mexico's nuclear enchantment is his extensive preparatory research, which surpasses the scouting done by most landscape photographers, even in this "age of questioning."[14] The site of the principal atomic blast—Trinity—was high on his list, but he hunted for two other historic atomic explosions which were conducted underground and constituted aspects of President Eisenhower's Plowshares Program under "Atoms for Peace." There was "Operation Gnome" on December 10, 1961, forty-eight kilometers southeast of Carlsbad, New Mexico, and "Project Gasbuggy" on December 10, 1967, in the Carson National Forest up around Farmington. To find the Gasbuggy site he traveled for seven hours on the "J" roads, dirt roads through the Jicarilla Apache reservation in the San Juan Basin Gas Field where there are natural gas deposits. By nightfall he was ready to give up, go home, and come back out another time and stay in a motel:

Plate 4

Suddenly there it was, with a marking so obscure, as if no one should see it. Nothing else there but one little plaque. . . . It says something like: "Project Gasbuggy 1961. With the cooperation of El Paso Gas and the Atomic Energy Commission a twenty-nine kiloton nuclear bomb was exploded to open up gas fields underground." Then it tells you, "No drilling more than fifteen hundred feet can be done within a one hundred foot radius of this plaque." Nothing's fenced off; so in other words, it's all hot under there. And the plaque is just like a grave marker. That's it; *that is it.* Most people in Farmington don't even know about the blast.[15]

Standing in the field's grassy stubble with piñon trees massed in the distance, Nagatani makes a grim frontal shot (Plate 4) in color with his 6-×-7 Pentax of the "grave marker" from an angle that shows in bronze the names of the "participants" in the project: "U.S. Atomic Energy Commission, U.S. Dept. of Interior (Bureau of Mines) El Paso Natural Gas Company." Back in the studio he begins the process of transformation by coloring the print selectively with transparent Marshall's oils and then collaging to this a colored vignette of a friend's arthritic hands, dyed blue and seeming to glow. The hands playfully cradle a family of rubber cockroaches painted to suggest their process of transformation, as if they were the last sentient beings on earth. Nagatani explains that his idea was to connect Kafka's nightmare of the colossal cockroach in "The Metamorphosis" with popular expectations from horror movies of mutations resulting from nuclear fallout, as in *Godzilla* or the giant ants in *Them*.[16] But the photographer also wanted to suggest other popular rumors, that after nuclear war the only survivors would be insects with hard shells impervious to atmospheric change.

The conception for *Ground Zero, "Operation Gnome"* (Plate 3) is a compositional variant of the Gasbuggy piece. At the Gnome site, which Nagatani found on an outing with friends to Carlsbad, quite by instinct along the "J" roads without a map, again he lets the plaque look abandoned by situating it in the far distance so that we might mistakenly confuse it with a broken television set or lone tombstone. Knowing that there had been a core leak of radioactive materials, nobody in Nagatani's group wanted to get out of the car. And so the photographer conveys the desolation of the place without a fence or danger signs to alert the public to the possibility of radioactive dust.

Plate 3

Back in the studio an assistant makes a 30-$\times$-40-inch chromogenic print. Then Nagatani paints the sky pink red like a sunset that has devoured the earth. From this miniature we jump across a nonexistent middle ground to a huge, infernal sacrifice in the foreground. The burning shape is like that of one of the cockroaches, now the scale of a beached whale. This unidentifiable "thing" is actually a group of sculptures by Shereen Lobdell that Nagatani saw exhibited in Albuquerque and obtained permission to set on fire in the gallery. He was struck by the subterranean mood of the pieces; like great incinerated beings after a nuclear war they looked like the dregs of past populations. And so he got the sculptor's permission to pour lighter fluid over them in a sand pile. He exposed a 4-$\times$-5 negative three times; for each subsequent exposure he added more lighter fluid to the flames so that every moment recorded was a different "fire" responding to a new ablution, the resultant print becoming a sort of flaming composite. Thus, Nagatani's diligent research into the facts behind his subject matter are profoundly inspiring, and led him almost instantaneously into elaborate and time-consuming theatrical manipulations in order to bring the images into being.

Nagatani says he gets a lot of his information about nuclear activity from the government, but what he collects on his own far surpasses in detail what he finds in the mail. Even this is not acquired simply to inform his pictures. Rather, he says he saved certain "facts" over the past three years, like information in a book on the effects of absinthe on French culture, in order to "remind" himself of layerings and associations of ideas he wanted the photographs to contain. With a child's absorption which mirrors that of the first nuclear physicists themselves, Nagatani researched, and started to tinker, inevitably losing himself in the loose wires of his subject.

At first, like his trips to the blast sites, his approach is entirely desultory, fueled by an incorrigible curiosity. The information turns up as randomly as reading the morning paper or thumbing through assorted magazines in the dentist's office or on flights between Albuquerque, Los Angeles, New York, and other parts of the country. He devours a history of rocketry by Robert Goddard, the "one-dream man," who in 1926 designed and built the world's first liquid-fueled rocket. He buys the premier issue of *Defense World,* The Magazine of Defense Issues and Technologies, which discusses "America's Weaponry: How Good is It?," "Modern Aerial Combat: High Stakes . . . High Risks," "International Cooperation: Option or Ultimatum?" or mysteriously "Invisible Weapons?—Stealth Technologies and Tactics." *Defense World*'s editorials assure him that "military operations, the seriousness of their mission notwithstanding, are exciting. So are the development, manufacture and testing of the weapons the defense industry produces to support them. . . . In return for the billions of dollars the U.S. and its allies spend on defense annually, the free world can go to sleep at night knowing deterrence works and the probability of nuclear war is very low."[17] Nagatani turns from this cheerful confidence to Robert Goodin's assertion that:

The balance of terror has kept the peace for the past thirty-five years . . . but thirty-five years is just too short a run on which to base our probability judgments, given the unacceptability of even very small probabilities of such a very great horror. Besides, nuclear war is just not the sort of thing whose probabilities we dare to estimate by trial-and-error procedures—the first error may well mark the learner's own end.[18]

The photographer turns to Jonathan Schell's *The Fate of the Earth,* which amplifies these logical absurdities with ferocious clarity: "a much less reassuring, much less frequently voiced, and much less defensible proposition . . . is that one prepares for extinction in order to protect national interests."[19] The reader finds out the degree to which we are already the recipients of the gift of nuclear trial and error, how we are already contaminated from within by gamma rays and beta particles and radioactive isotopes in fallout, the two most dangerous being strontium 90 which has a half-life of twenty-eight years, and cesium 137 with a half-life of thirty years. Strontium 90 resembles calcium and makes its way in the body to the bones where it is thought to cause cancer. As Schell states: "Every person in the world now has in his bones a measurable deposit of strontium 90 traceable to the fallout from atmospheric nuclear testing."[20]

These are starters. The photographer reads McGeorge Bundy's *Danger and Survival: Choices About the Bomb* and John Newhouse's *War and Peace in the Nuclear Age.* He finds in Helen Caldicott's *Missile Envy* "information that loads you to a gloom. Effective!—that's part of it, that's very important." He passes to Luther Carter's *Nuclear Imperatives and Public Trust,* and to *The Nuclear Waste Primer: A Handbook for Citizens* put out by the League of Women Voters' Education Fund.

He tries to fill in a form that helps citizens determine their "Average, Natural, Personal Radiation Dose." He finds out that the average annual dose is 180 millirems, but the form says it is not uncommon for people to receive far more in a given year. "This is not dangerous," he is assured. "As an example, exposure to 5,000 mrems is allowed for those who work with and around radioactive material." To determine your mrem dose, to "26—cosmic radiation at sea level," "add 40" if you live at 7,000 feet; "add 7" if your house is stone, concrete, or masonry; "add 24" for the US mrem average in food, water, and air; "add 4" for "weapons test fallout." For each 2,500 miles of jet plane travel annually, "add 1 mrem"; for each hour of TV over a year's time "multiply the total by .15." Then the form notes, "One mrem per year is equal to increasing your diet by 4% or by taking a five-day hike in the Sierra Nevada mountains." Nagatani discovers that his number of millirems is considerably over 180. And then he doesn't know how many mrems he should add for his repeated dustings when he visited the Trinity site, or the village of Paguate at the Laguna Pueblo, or Church Rock, or Shiprock, or Radium

Springs, or Mortandad Canyon, or the "Operation Gnome" site or that of "Project Gasbuggy," or the Rio Puerco near Gallup. The form croons back at him, "We live in a radioactive world—always have."[21] But how radioactive? The photographer wonders.

What Nagatani can do about his exposure is not within the power of the form to convey. Maybe this is why he decides to begin using the old civil defense Geiger counter sent to him by a physicist, turned photographer, Greg MacGregor. Although he creates farcical explosions himself from which he makes "nuclear" images, MacGregor is genuinely worried about the radioactive dust on his friend's shoes. (Nagatani memorizes the contents of the instruction manual.)

Maybe this is why he also saves an article in *National Geographic* on atomic radioactivity still in the soil of Bikini in the Marshall Islands of Micronesia, where on July 1, 1946, the B-29 bomber *Dave's Dream* initiated nuclear testing in the Pacific, maneuvers which rendered Bikini and other surrounding islands still virtually unlivable forty-five years later. On television he sees interviews with the navy men who continue to suffer slow and painful death by gradually losing legs and arms and finally succumbing from the effects of massive radiation at Bikini about which they were so ill informed. He learns that on a subsequent test of a fifteen-megaton bomb on Bikini in March 1954, "small animals were found to have suffered retinal burns at a distance of three hundred and forty-five miles."[22]

In patrolling the activities of the air force through the press, he discovers that a large nuclear arsenal is tucked under the Manzano Mountains and guarded by the air force at the Kirtland base. He shoots this mountain storage place as it would be observed on a daily basis by its nearest neighbors in the local population, through a cyclone fence over the ubiquitous flames of a home barbecue, which he gets permission to set up in a neighboring yard (Plate 21). Then on the set he strings up a couple of tiny F-16 Falcons from the Air Force Thunderbird Performance Team, positioning them so that they seem to entertain their backyard audience by skimming along the edge of the barbed wire and disappearing into the blue beyond. This is an oblique way of identifying the actual subject of the nuclear cache, which is, of course, never shown except as the mound of dirt that interrupts the horizon, beneath which, in fact, lies the warhead storage area. Thus, it is not without a certain irony that he clips a report on the arrest over the past

Plate 21

eight years of "fourteen members of an elite Air Force security unit assigned to guard nuclear weapons at Kirtland . . . who have been arrested and convicted of drug charges."[23]

He discovers that southeast of the main runway of the Albuquerque International Airport is a wooden monstrosity called the Trestle, which simulates electromagnetic impulses to a degree that worries public interest groups in Washington, D.C., not to mention the citizens of Albuquerque. This massive structure made of six million board feet of wood is large enough to support not only a B1 bomber, but the nation's largest military plane, the mammoth C-5 Galaxy transport, which weighs 550,000 pounds. These aircraft are subjected to electromagnetic pulses (EMP) of the kind that would be produced by an atmospheric nuclear explosion, in order to test the aircraft's strength, "to harden" them.

The photographer reads in the *Albuquerque Tribune* that the great horned owl community roosting in the Trestle have been raising owlets "like crazy." "Heck, it's a darned good habitat," says Captain David Shaw, a weapons laboratory information officer and avid bird watcher. The owls and the C-5 Galaxy survive the EMPs well, but the groups worried about being exposed to harmful electromagnetic fields learn that the Trestle is only one of five Kirtland simulators at the airport. Each creates an EMP environment which allows aircraft to see if they can "crank up" and fly in a feigned nuclear blast: "That's what we learn out here."[24]

The article is the first inspiration for *Simulation/Simulation, The Trestle, Nuclear Effects (Electromagnetic Pulses) Simulation Facility, Air Force Weapons Laboratory, Kirtland Air Force Base, Albuquerque, New Mexico,* 1990 (Plate 17) in which Nagatani shows another "darned good habitat," his own kitchen, meant to be equally dubious. He observes with a smile, "Like living in hell, right?" The kitchen spoofs in every way skewed notions of safety in laboratories and facilities that "feign" nuclear blasts and electromagnetic pulses. The TV, carrying in lurid blue an image of the Trestle made by nuclear information expert Robert Del Tredici, as well as the microwave oven, which also throws out electromagnetic impulses, signal our attention.[25] Then there is Nagatani's own *metal* version of the Trestle, not only totally out of scale, built from an old erector set his father gave

16

him, but meant to be ridiculous, its very metal materials exposing the blithe ignorance of the hobbyist.

Among the flowered curtains and disconcerting pink purple glow, which seems to leak from the user-friendly appliances, Nagatani displays his own hand-built arsenal of aeronautical symbols.[26] The little planes are his passion; here he lays them out as his own cottage industry, but they also function as a table of contents for identifying the cast of characters in the other images of the series.[27] The big silver B-36 on the impossible metal "trestle" in the foreground is the type of plane that dropped an accidental H-bomb on Albuquerque in 1957, a subject which consumes him and from which he will create a stern, troubling scenario (Plate 20).The F-16s with red tails on top of the TV appeared in his shot of the nuclear arsenal in the Manzano mountains (Plate 21). The Stealth fighter shows up in the Chaco Canyon shot (Plate 38). An F-111 is on the table at the left. Another appears on the microwave with an A7-D, which recurs in the Kirtland Air Force shot (Plate 16). In this playful evocation of terror through toys, the mushrooms are the only representatives of nature. Trailing bits of dirt, they dot the terrain of the still life like simulated atomic clouds, their heads and supermarket convenience shapes suggesting dreadful little push buttons.

Plate 17

Nagatani discovers through reading about the Trestle that simulated testing by the military is à la mode. On June 2, 1989, he reads about "Miser's Gold," the chemical blast of 2,400 tons of ammonium nitrate and fuel oil at White Sands that also has been designed to simulate the effects of a nuclear explosion.[28] But this is child's play. The reported activity is one thing. What interests Nagatani more is what gets hidden.

He begins to follow the trail of other gumshoes—defense writers for the *Albuquerque Journal* like David H. Morrissey. This journalist also reports on espionage in New Mexico since it seems to be an American tradition practically established with the Trinity test. He discusses the case of atomic spy Klaus Fuchs among several other celebrated cases of Soviet spying, notably that of Julius and Ethel Rosenberg. From this Nagatani turns to Robert Chadwell Williams's book-length account of the intricate network of spies around atomic secrets which elaborates the story of the two matching parts of a Jello package that Harry Gold used to make contact with David Greenglass in their campaign to pass along nuclear secrets in the form of rough plans for Fat Man and Little Boy to the Rosenbergs.[29]

Nagatani makes a note about the Jello packages thinking that the graphics would look good in a shot. He's luckier with this shot than he anticipated. He begins with a few false starts using two women in red dresses in a motel, which doesn't convey the dour loneliness of the enterprise of "secrets," especially among the spies on the lowest echelons of the couriers for the Russian military.[30] But one day driving in downtown Albuquerque he passes the house at 209 High Street, where Greenglass stayed, and decides to knock on the door. A Mrs. Freeman there not only assures him that "this is the spy place," but shows him her "spy" scrapbook of news clippings and lets him into number 4, Greenglass's former apartment, which is conveniently unoccupied.

Plate 31

What a grim scenario Nagatani fabricates from the little High Street kitchen under the eaves with its dirty tan walls and rick-rack-trimmed curtains (Plate 31). Unlike the lavishly colored work with Tracey, this kind of staging is closer to Nagatani's dreaming in *Nuclear Enchantment.* Not that he is incapable of losing himself in a full palette of color. Rather, here the utter banality of the place inspires him. He adds the globe, the rough simulated drawings for Fat Man and Little Boy, drawing paraphernalia, and of course, the thirty-one packages of cherry Jello, a motif, the mere repetition of which lifts the scene out of the supremely ordinary into the demimonde of "a spy place." Nagatani picks cherry Jello for reasons of his own. It is one of the earliest Jello flavors, he tells me, but also it reminds him of children's innocent, round, red cherry bombs with their little green fuse stems. The Jello is also a sexual target for the photographer. The "cherries," brightening up the setting into which he has us peer, as if from behind a curtain, act as a kind of lure and suggest that spying and sex have always had a secret equality.

Nagatani also photocopies pages from Senator Clinton P. Anderson's memoirs, which spill the beans on additional Air Force indifference to elementary safety precautions with nuclear weapons by accidently dropping a hydrogen bomb "in a pile of dirt just outside Albuquerque."[31] He soon discovers that David Morrissey has been tracking this cover-up for years. In 1986 the journalist publishes the first details concerning the accident. Nagatani is held in their grip:

The H-Bomb accidentally fell out of a B-36 bomber coming in to land at Kirtland Air Force Base on May 22, 1957. The bomber was at an altitude of 1,700 feet when the 42,000-pound Mark 17 bomb dropped from the aircraft ripping off the bomb bay doors. Although the weapon was not fully armed at the time of the accident it did contain conventional nonnuclear high explosives and radioactive nuclear materials such as plutonium. The bomb plunged from the aircraft and smashed into the ground approximately 4¹/₂ miles south of Kirtland's control tower—some 5¹/₂ miles south of Gibson Boulevard. There was no nuclear explosion and no one was injured. But the bomb's nonnuclear explosives detonated, blasting a crater "approximately 25 feet in diameter and 12 feet deep," government documents say. . . . Government documents revealed the bomb was 625 times more powerful than the one dropped on Hiroshima. . . . The accident happened when the plane hit turbulence and another crew member, trying to keep from falling, accidently grabbed the release mechanism that releases the bomb.

Plate 20

Morrissey interviews the pilot of a small plane in flight that day who remembers that it wasn't turbulent at all, but "a beautiful, clear, smooth May morning."[32]

Nagatani feeds on the contradictions like a glutton. The facts that Morrissey brings together from one article to the next take on the magnitude of myth. Nagatani memorizes the number of tons, the distance in miles, the amount of plutonium, the number of times more powerful than the bomb at Hiroshima. Poised like "Mr. Memory" he recites the facts as if in a trance. The amazing revelations rivet his curiosity, stimulate an already well-honed instinct for the absurd. The details are the life's blood of his art. What excites him about the documentation of nuclear activity in the popular press is that even the most dispassionate report seems far-fetched, too impossible to believe. The facts read like a dream. "Our knowledge is . . . vast, and . . . what we know is extremely alarming," Jonathan Schell observed.[33] Nagatani has no choice but to believe it. Out of his network of public information, he invents a photographic monument to help him ponder the alarm.

On a windy October afternoon in 1990 he invites a group of people to accompany him to the site of the H-bomb dropping near the Albuquerque Airport in order to make *The Accident* (Plate 20). To each person he has assigned a role. Three are to be news gatherers, with press cameras, notebooks, and stern glances. Two will play photographers. One, using a beautiful view camera of cherry wood and brass that he built himself, is to be absorbed in recording a Pueblo Indian family which seems to have gathered near the accident site. (In fact, the group is a color photograph that Nagatani mounted on foam-core board.) Another photographer, wearing a Hawaiian shirt, kneels down with a reflex camera as if to photograph a nude woman whom Nagatani instructs to imitate the nudes in California dune landscapes of the 1930s by Edward Weston. Following his directions she has difficulty avoiding the scrub cactus that covers the site.

Photograph: Eugenia P. Janis.

Earlier in the day the photographer visited the site with a shovel. He dug a hole to approximate the original "pile of dirt" and poured green paint over it marking the spot of the disaster. Now he arranges two other photos on foam core of gesturing women in military uniforms who embrace the width of the depression in the earth like two parentheses. The airplane responsible for the accident soars over the tableau like a ship in trouble. In fact, it is Nagatani's hand-built model of the B-36 suspended from an aluminum stand on nylon monofilament. This prop presents one of the most serious impediments to making the shot. The day is so windy that the plane won't hold still; amidst the roar, the actors try to hold their expressions while listening to the photographer's instructions; and a technical assistant surveying the group through the camera mounted on high on a tripod tries to stand on a rickety box without collapsing it.

Photograph: Eugenia P. Janis.

Nagatani prints the scene and isn't satisfied. The issues are not clear, there's not enough distance. Besides, the fact of the accidental H-bomb dropping on Albuquerque is not the only thing that interests him. It is also the way we come to know about the event. There is no readily available official pictorial record from the actual day of the accident. Almost three decades later the press publishes a picture of a depression in the ground (presumably made by the bomb) with some assigned "investigator" pointing to it. The very nature of the cover-up requires that the "events," such as they are twenty-five years later, be *reshot,* and necessarily reinvented.

And so Nagatani, dressed in army fatigues, also returns to the airport landscape, now covered with snow. In the bitter December cold he locates the depression he had dug in the fall, sets up the shot, and holds the image, this time from a position facing the airport and the Sandia Mountains. The result perfectly conveys the strange fictions that emerge in the validity claimed for evidence captured by press pictures. In the process of reshooting, the view camera records its own shadow on his back, a fortuitous sign that Nagatani enjoys. It also records the pristine purity of the land during an exceptionally cold New Mexico December, a photographic fact that only temporarily obscures the occult toxicity of this "nuclear winter," which the photographer brings into view by printing the sky an ashen pink.

The newspaper accounts that he reads daily increasingly amaze him by virtue of their reasonable intention to inform. An article tells that soon an 800-page history of the Sandia National Laboratories will be published because few in New Mexico "can offer any detailed explanation of what this economic giant, which employs 7,200 people and spends in a year more than 1 billion dollars, does."[34] He clips a piece on the air force's plan to build a giant telescope, which will be operational in 1992, and capable of seeing objects the size of a basketball 1,000 miles in space. "Researchers will use the telescope to make the stars stop twinkling."[35] He revels in the Associated Press's perfect aplomb: "A Nuke Attack Wouldn't Halt Tax Man." The manual that guides the conduct of all IRS employees acknowledges that tax collection might suffer if the bomb is dropped but that "once the emergency is over, within 30 days" the agency would expect to resume assessing and collecting, and in "unimpaired areas" still be going after delinquent accounts.[36]

Then there is the New Mexico story, "Huge Yucca Found at White Sands Missile Range Sets Record." Nagatani clips this too. The plant is twenty-three feet five inches tall and has a five-foot circumference. Its competitor in the state measures only four feet. The yucca's great height can't be explained, but people at White Sands are joking about the possible influence of radiation from nuclear tests on the range since World War II. "The plant predates the Trinity explosion and is supposed to have survived the blast from its position ten miles away," muses Nagatani. "Or did it get a growth spurt from all that testing at White Sands?"[37] Either way, the specimen is a lot bigger than it ought to be, and tough enough to have survived what tens of thousands of Japanese did not. He considers doing a photograph about the yucca, but in the end other ideas take over.

For example, *Air Force Magazine* tells of Dr. Lytle S. Adams, a dental surgeon from Irwin, Pennsylvania, who decided, shortly after the Japanese bombed Pearl Harbor in 1941, that America could "fight back" by utilizing the millions of bats at Carlsbad Caverns. He proposed fitting the bats with tiny incendiary bombs in oblong nitrocellulose cases filled with thickened kerosene to which was attached a small time-delay igniter. President Roosevelt approved the plan, and the research went ahead. The initial tests, using 3,500 armed bats dropped from a B-29 flying 5,000 feet, failed since most of the bats, which had to be "cooled" down to force them into hibernation for transport to the airfield, died on impact, most of them still asleep during the experiment. But many other experiments on Project X-Ray continued into 1944. In one that led to the army ceding control to the navy, the bats escaped wearing live incendiaries and set fire to a hangar and to the general's car. By 1944 when it aborted, Project X-Ray had cost some 2 million dollars and over 6,000 bats.[38]

The higher intelligence of Dr. Adams's bats inspires *"Fin de Siècle" Bat Flight Amphitheater* (Plate 39), where the photographer envisions Carlsbad not only as a guana haven, but a place where humans take second place, wear gas masks to survive, and warn others. Here the little fliers are radioactive screamers drowning out the clacking of the Geiger counter held by the photographer, an allusion to the invasion of nuclear garbage in the salt pits of the Waste Isolation Pilot Plant (WIPP) being "tested" for safety nearby and the possibility that the kingdom of bats might reign in splendid isolation into the twenty-first century.

The newspaper and magazine articles become comic relief for the photographer's profound capacity for astonishment. "If I were an alien I'd want to explore what's going on in that little place called New Mexico." Nagatani reflects:

Plate 39

New Mexico has this kind of mystery about it. Holloman Air Force Base is the place where the most UFO citings in the world have taken place. There's a book called the *The Roswell Incident* which explains that in 1947 they confiscated the remnants of an alien aircraft that came down, found the bodies of several aliens, and put them in the hangar. It's a famous case. All

these guys took lie detector tests. But it never came out in the press. Over forty years later all we get is heresay.[39]

There's another case at Holloman Air Force Base where the retiring base commander finally admitted that for three years they had an alien "guest" on the base. The commandant of the base retires and finally says: "Now I can tell you."

And so when he makes *Passage of Time, Unidentified Flying Objects* (Plate 23), the photographer shows, at the entrance to Holloman Air Force Base, a tall soldier who wants us to look at something he's spotted up in the blue. It isn't the trio of F-15s from the Forty-Ninth TAC Fighter Wing that crowns the scene from visible monofilament supports, nor is it the silver "alien" that slinks out of the picture. Nor does the pointing man see the "gorilla." He's seen something else. But who knows what? Like the retiring commandant, the soldier is, quite literally, in a position to "tell." The gorilla seems to be a dissonant nonsequitur in the arrangement, but the photographer reveals that he put it there not only to represent a stage in the evolutionary history of man, but to stand for Holloman's lesser-known monkey testing program. In addition to being the place where there have been more unidentified flying objects sighted than anywhere else in New Mexico, a laboratory at Holloman has been "sighted" by certain animal protection organizations for its questionable experiments on chimpanzees.

Plate 23

Besides the wondrous tales of air force activity, what Nagatani patrols most in New Mexico is the detection and clean-up of toxic nuclear waste. The EPA sends him a quarterly status report of "Superfund Sites," which describes aquifer contamination around the state from metal recovery mills, railroad yards, lead, zinc, and copper mills. It cites the Homestake Mining Company near Milan, in Cibola County, which was an active uranium mill with 22 million tons of tailings that cover an estimated 245 acres piled up to 100 feet high. These have begun seeping into an aquifer under the site.[40] Nagatani's perspective on tailings preceded his settling in New Mexico:

If you're on the right side of a Southwest Airlines 737 heading west and look out (if you're not over the wing) you see beautiful white deposits below that

make a striking contrast with the grey brown landscape. I have to laugh to myself when I hear people around me admiring these "natural" formations. They're uranium tailing deposits, acres and acres of them. They're all hot, they're all radioactive.

From this he concocts a queer "barnyard" scene, within sight of Mount Taylor, which shows the rusting remnants of the Homestake Mining Company that operated near Milan and Grants, New Mexico, in the 1950s (Plate 5). He makes the sky yellow, a leitmotif for "yellow cake," the nickname for the ore of the milling process that Homestake crushed, ground, chemically treated, and then shipped off to be converted into uranium hexafluoride, which in a gaseous state was further enriched and turned into solid uranium dioxide. This entered the fuel pads of nuclear reactors in the form of ceramic pellets. The only animal life in the place is a big Guernsey dropping a cow pie (drawn as if by a twelve year old, and sitting at the animal's feet), which alludes to the debris of the "yellow cake" process. The cow is a prize-winning milker that Nagatani found at the New Mexico State Fair. He wanted its scale to loom large, much in the way the great draftsman Hiroshige did with a large horse standing in its own dung in the *One Hundred Famous Views of Edo*.[41]

Plate 5

Nagatani photocopies an article on the United Nuclear Corporation's cleanup of the 900-acre Church Rock uranium mining site used from 1977 to 1982, which is estimated to take ten years and some 25 million dollars to complete. Despite this the Rio Puerco, which carries water along Interstate 40 in western New Mexico and eastern Arizona, is contaminated with ten to one hundred times the maximum allowable level of radioactivity.[42] He goes to an EPA public information hearing at Church Rock to learn firsthand about the cleanup at the United Nuclear Corporation there. He starts talking to one of the participants at the hearing and asks him how this situation differs from the Homestake Mining area in Milan and Grants.

Plate 9

As our conversation went on, he started to get a little bit anxious because he wondered, "Who is this guy?" In fact he asked me, "How do you know all this stuff?" which is all public information, but no one really goes through

 24

all the work of finding this out. I think I actually made him nervous because I knew the *extent* of what was going on. He wanted to know my credentials and what I was doing, which I told him. And that was fine. It didn't seem to him like a threat. I told him I was an artist. I taught at UNM, that I was doing a body of work on the landscape in New Mexico specific to nuclear issues, and I imagine that what immediately ran through his mind when I said I was an artist was "Oh my God, some kind of leftist!" But in a way I think he also thought, "Well, pictures can't hurt; he's not going to be on television or writing in the newspaper. So OK."

Nagatani keeps a brochure on nuclear fuels technology at Los Alamos because its text and glossy color illustrations have the assertive confidence of a corporate annual report. He likes the look. It reminds him of his own pictures, and he decides he wants to get more of that look into his work.

He receives the U.S. Department of Energy's silver-covered brochure on the WIPP site. From Sandia National Laboratories he obtains a publication entitled "The Scientific Program at the Waste Isolation Pilot Plant" which explains "transuranic [element heavier than uranium—that is, plutonium] waste" and their dangers, the hazards of radioactivity and the thousands of years it remains hazardous.[43] "The Atomic bomb is shit," Oppenheimer once said. He realized soon enough that radioactive wastes were filthy insults against the proper order of things.[44]

Nagatani clips maps from the newspapers that plot the locations that will ship nuclear waste into New Mexico to the Waste Isolation Pilot Plant (WIPP) twenty-six miles east of Carlsbad and remembers the bats. He also determines exactly what kinds of "trash" will be transported to the massive underground salt beds. He reads that the trash will be shipped in TRUPACT II containers, each of which will hold fourteen fifty-gallon drums of waste. Each of these drums will contain more than fifteen grams of "remarkably toxic" plutonium of which one-millionth of a gram can cause cancer.[45]

He concocts *WIPP Nuclear Crossroads, U.S. 285, 60, 54, Vaughn, New Mexico,* 1989 (Plate 37) from images he's collected from the press. A truck carrying TRUPACT II containers of radioactive waste heads south down Route

285 under sulphuric skies. It passes a roadside plaque describing "Vaughn, population 737, elevation 5,965" which reads:

Vaughn, a division point in the transcontinental railway system, is located along the route of the Stinson cattle trail. In 1882, Jim Stinson, manager of the New Mexico Land and Livestock Co., drove 20,000 cattle in eight separate herds along this important trail from Texas to the Estancia Valley.

Plate 37

Along this historically important trail today there are no cattle. By collaging three corpses of the roadrunner, New Mexico's state bird, along the highway, the photographer makes it clear that the land along Route 285 is no longer a place for any living creatures.

Then he fantasizes about a WIPP accident, for the newspaper articles about possible spills read like a storybook. "All they've told us is that if there is an emergency, we call this special number and someone will be here in an hour and a half," a young woman is reported as saying. "But what if there's a wreck, and the driver is pinned in the cab or something? Even if I don't know whether the site is contaminated, I'm not going to sit around for an hour and a half."[46]

In *WIPP TRUPACT II Accident, Atomic Auto Wreckers, Near Las Cruces, New Mexico,* 1990 (Plate 36) the photographer shows us a "wreck," which we view from inside the relative safety of a truck cab, its windows smeared with New Mexico clay. Outside three men discuss an "accident." One who looks like a state policeman holds a double-barreled shotgun. Another sheathed like a pupa in yellow coveralls and a gas mask gestures as if he knows more than the others. Under his arm Nagatani has collaged an oversized official-looking "Contamination Checklist" taken from a Department of Energy pamphlet. In the background three TRUPACT II containers of radioactive waste teeter on a presumably wrecked truck that's been towed in for repairs to some local garage called "Atomic Auto Wrecking," which also fixes foreign cars.

Plate 36

Nagatani xeroxes the Department of Energy's published tabulations of the cost of cleanup for nuclear weapons complexes at Los Alamos; Lawrence Livermore National Laboratory; the Nevada Test Site; the Savannah River Plant in Aiken, South Carolina, which produces plutonium and tritium; the Y-12 Plant in Oakridge,

26

Tennessee; Rocky Flats in Golden, Colorado; and the Pantex Plant in Amarillo, Texas. He keeps public relations brochures from the Idaho National Engineering Laboratory which describe its various breeder reactors and transuranic waste management. Most of these facilities will be sending high-level waste to the proposed WIPP site. When the photographer sees these sites laid out on a map of the United States, they span the whole continent and show clearly how many places are sending nuclear waste to New Mexico. "They're saving the best for the last," Nagatani smiles.

PATRICK'S FIREBALL THEATER: AN EMPIRE OF SIGNS

As a Catholic Japanese-American who grew up in a Polish neighborhood in Chicago, Nagatani's curiosity about where he lives has to do with feeling for a long time that he didn't really belong anywhere. Today his parents practice Buddhism, but he sees their renewed need for religious authenticity as an acquisiton of advancing years. Nonetheless, he is grateful for it since he remembers spending much of his life hardly knowing where or how he was supposed to fit in. He didn't learn to use chopsticks until he was in high school. He visited Europe before he even considered Japan. Now when he's in Japan, he feels supremely anonymous in "a sea of black-haired people." But the natives are astonished when he can't understand them or answer back when someone speaks to him. "Everything about me consists of a kind of layering. At home I put Japanese rice on the same table with meatloaf. . . . Also, I've worn glasses since I was five; being a 'four eyes' established the secret feeling that underneath it all, I was an outcast."

He's proud to belong to the Atomic Photographers' Guild, but he sticks out there too, especially when they inform him he's the only photographer in the group who "uses metaphor." The guild includes documentors, such as its founder Robert Del Tredici and Carole Gallagher, funded by the MacArthur Foundation, who recorded radiogenic health effects on the population living downwind of the Nevada Test Site in a book called *Nuclear Towns: The Secret War in the American West.* Among the others, Japanese photographer Kenji Higuchi has been documenting the nuclear power industry in Japan for sixteen years; Yoshito Matsushige, a newspaper photographer and army reporter living in Hiroshima when the bomb exploded, took five pictures on that day from within the city; Hiromitsu Toyosaki, another Japanese photojournalist, documents radiation victims in the Marshall Islands and Native American uranium miners of New Mexico and Arizona, as well as the "downwinders" of southern Utah, residents of Three Mile Island, and Australian atomic veterans. Gunter Zint documents the nuclear politics of repression in Germany as evidenced by the police's destruction of "anti-atom villages" built by thousands of people opposed to nuclear technologies scheduled for Brokdorf and Gorleben. Through this group Nagatani exhibited his nuclear work in Berlin in the fall of 1990, and his pictures traveled throughout Germany in 1991 for the World Uranium Hearings.

What constitutes Nagatani's "metaphor" in the *Enchantment* pictures? His colors and staged setups have always seemed aggressively comical and bombastic, but in Germany the new work glowed with a special phosphorescence against the black-and-white field shots of human misery and injustice by the other Atomic Guild photographers. Nagatani's new stagings are paste-ups of a layered language of signs. The many images within a single work act as vectors that point toward collisions of ideas which he calculates to look ridiculous in order more effectively to tell the truth; this is in contrast to the multitude of reading he has done in the press, which, despite its good faith, seems to him to perform the opposite function.

From the fireball theater that originated at Trinity, Nagatani has created his own. The forms of the first pictures fabricated are undeniably rooted in the earlier photographs done with Andrée Tracey. In fact some of the figures in the initial pictures for the series he had already staged with her in 1986 before he arrived in New Mexico. Now with her permission he recycles them. For these big shots he uses the biggest of the six different studios in Albuquerque that he employed for this project.[47] Actually the first pictures are not only linked compositionally but repeat certain motifs and formats among themselves which reinforce certain ideas.

In one of these early conceptions, which introduces the series, Nagatani shows himself, armed with a black umbrella, exploring Ground Zero at the Trinity Site (Plate 1) and trying to avoid being pulverized by a storm of green gaseous rock, a form of glass, called Trinitite, produced from the sand and great heat in the Trinity blast. (Actually, fearing Trinitite's radioactivity the material was dumped into a lead building on the site.) Andrée Tracey painted dozens of styrofoam pieces different shades of green and suspended them from translucent monofilament so that a Trinitite storm appears to swirl across the desolate mountains, around the grim monument with its commemorative plaques, and to clobber the poor photographer.

Artists introduce themselves as authors of their work in many ways, especially in the history of the graphic arts. It is interesting to compare to the present frontispiece the self-portrait that Francesco Goya made to lead off the *Caprichos*, a series of compositions in etching and aquatint which expose the moral breakdown of Spanish institutions and society generally at the end of the eighteenth century through a series of veiled metaphors. Goya's top hat and appraising glance assure us that he is equipped with all he needs to contrive the "caprices," which are simply intelligence, detachment, and two good eyes. But the artist's glance also reveals someone weary from seeing too much, a demeanor that sheds light on the bewildered face of Nagatani.

In the Trinitite portrait all of the photographer's observing faculties seem threatened. We can hardly find him under the protective gear. He wears the glasses he always wears, but he's added a respirator to help him breathe. Over this, a protective costume (built by his wife, Jeanean Bodwell), hermetically sealed to repel extreme heat and radioactivity, covers him from head to toe. The plastic reflection of the helmet nearly obscures his glance, which focuses downward as if fearing to step on something that might blow him up, reduce him to another Trinitite pellet.

Plate 1

Despite these encumbrances the artist appears determined to carry on his research. He looks like he is being lowered underwater. In this image he is, above all, a kind of nuclear scout. His disappearing figure speaks eloquently of the life-threatening circumstances that surround him. Yet everything alludes to an older tradition, that of the artist as the romantic traveler instinctively turning to nature for solace. But what a distortion of the former ideal, which of course is the point. The way Nagatani furtively clutches the umbrella flaunts its inadequacy. As a symbol it encapsulates what the doomsayers refer to as "prenuclear thinking," much as suntan lotion did for Dr. Teller just before the first atomic bomb went off.

In another of the early large-scale constructions, Nagatani explores a similar theme of human vulnerability in a group of Japanese people visiting the National Atomic Museum, at Kirtland Air Force Base (Plate 18). Here the figures wear Japanese clothing, and some eat sushi with chopsticks. Nobody sits down to the meal; rather like the stereotype, they are Japanese perpetually on tour. For the players Nagatani again uses himself, along with his mother and father, a niece and a nephew. The larger-than-life figure in the foreground is his brother's mother-in-law.

How complacent these bourgeoisie seem in their clean cotton kimonos and lacquered plates of rice with fish languishing in the *Twilight of the Raw.*[48] Nagatani's father, John, holds a California roll between chopsticks. His mother, Diane, nibbles yellowtail on a torpedo of rice. The photographer himself gazes at a Snark missile while between two chopsticks he holds a rice bullet striped with tuna.

Plate 18

Everyone's faces and hands blaze red, as if mirroring the light of exploding supernovas. The source of light is clarified by the looming appearance of Nagatani's brother's mother-in-law who looks toward something outside the picture as if it were talking to her. Clues to what it is are shown reflected in the mushroom clouds that fog the lenses of her glasses. Everyone in the shot, even the children, wears spectacles of some kind, not necessarily to see better but perhaps as a misconceived protection against the blazing light, just as Nagatani used the umbrella and Teller spread on suntan lotion against radiation. Even if some of the sushi eaters focus on the missile display overhead, Nagatani suggests a contrast between a Japanese way of life, even by Japanese-Americans, and the hallowed halls dedicated to the icons of warfare which they survey.

The imagery in this scene also touches on something exquisitely subtle about human frailty. It reinforces the mock reverence for military shrines that Nagatani alluded to in the Trinitite picture and exploits in another form the meaning held by the umbrella. Here the human symbol lies in the presence of the chopsticks, homely tools that one eminent observer found to be revealing signifyers within Japanese culture. Roland Barthes's little book deconstructing Japan devotes an entire chapter to chopsticks that makes a distinction between Western table cutlery which pierce, cut, slit, and wound, and chopsticks which he characterizes as instruments of culinary nonviolence.

By pointing to the food, "(and thus selecting there and then *this* and not *that*), [the chopstick] introduces into the use of the food not an order but a caprice, a certain indolence: in any case, an intelligent and no longer mechanical operation." Furthermore in the gesture of chopsticks, further softened by their substance—wood or lacquer—where "the foodstuff never undergoes a pressure greater than is precisely necessary to raise and carry it . . . there is something maternal, the same precisely measured care taken in moving a child: a force . . . no longer a pulsion. . . . In all their gestures the chopsticks never violate the foodstuff," rather they "prod it into separate pieces . . . thereby rediscovering the natural fissures of the substance. Their loveliest function is to *transfer* the food . . . they are the alimentary instrument which refuses . . . to mutilate. . . . Maternal they tirelessly perform the gesture which creates the mouthful, leaving to our alimentary manners, armed with pikes and knives, that of predation."[49] Nagatani has filled the space behind the sushi eaters with military tools "of predation" which cross each other like mammoth cutlery carving up a roasted sky. Thus, like the umbrella, the chopsticks become touching human deterrents against monstrous scientific defenses.

Other compositions originating in Nagatani's larger studio which bear traces of the collaboration with Tracey are the scenarios of *Trinity Site, Jornada del Muerto, New Mexico,* 1989 (Plate 2); *The Nike Hercules Missile Monument, Highway 70, White Sands Missile Range, New Mexico,* 1989 (Plate 26); and *"Lysistratus," National Atomic Museum, Albuquerque, New Mexico,* 1989 (Plate 19). In all of these the artist again employs real people whom he directs to be photographed and whose figures he later cuts and pastes onto cardboard stage flats to be set against other photographed and painted site shots.

Plate 2

In *Trinity Site, Jornada del Muerto, New Mexico* (Plate 2) the Asian man and little girl happened to be in front of the monument by chance. Nagatani collaged a perfectly proportioned photograph of his model of the *Enola Gay* into the child's hand and suspended it overhead from nylon monofilament for the final shot. Again, as with the Trinitite and sushi compositions, the Japanese are Nagatani's favorite comedians. Risking a good dusting in the premier landscape of radioactivity, which Nagatani makes glow a torrid red in the studio, they raise their cameras to the paltry stone pyramid with its grim bronze plaque as only the stereotypical Japanese tourist knows how to pay homage. Yet their gestures honor a force that caused grievous suffering among their own people. What is so arresting in this scene is the way the tourists turn to include the viewers, as if we too had to be part of the sacred adoring circle. "If you aren't, you'd better be," suggests the glance of the man on the right, reminding us of the dormant coercion in so many groups of "the faithful."

Plate 26

At the Nike-Hercules Missile Monument (Plate 26) the Japanese are at it again, having left their recreational vehicles to bring miniature missiles to the sacred shrine on Highway 70 as Buddhist pilgrims might bring little statues of Buddha to be blessed by revered spiritual teachers at the site. Here in a sanctuary of airless red hue at White Sands, the land is almost completely subsumed by fumes of an unknown origin. The only oracle is the missile itself; its streamlined silhouette is past wisdom, knowledge, or understanding. There is nothing left to do but worship the thing, or as one man does in the preeminent act of modern affirmation, to photograph it.

"Lysistratus" (Plate 19) updates an ancient theme where women discontinue sexual union with their partners until these men stop going to war. Nagatani shows the missiles at the National Atomic Museum as static, repellent silhouettes. It is the women who have taken to the skies. Ten nudes, photographed separately, Nagatani cut and pasted to look as if they, in their gracious youthfulness, were new aircraft populating the atmosphere. All turn their backs and with arms raised ascend heavenward, despite the lurid space with its abhorrent blanket of clouds. The bodies of the women are significant in not attempting to seduce. In their chaste postures they look ordinary, yet they are completely preoccupied by something of greater significance, their mission. The fact that we cannot see their faces makes the point clearly enough. They appear to multiply by themselves and through their numbers declare an unarguable position.

Plate 19

Spencer R. Weart observed in *Nuclear Fear* that in the polling done to determine opposition to nuclear reactors the striking difference between men and women on the subject was that "twice as many men as women came up with talk of progress and economic benefits; twice as many women as men spoke anxiously about dangers."[50] One woman in Nagatani's arrangement looks our way and with an unmistakable gesture calls a halt. It is no accident that the name on her military uniform, which even sports a medal, is shown to be "Geiger,"[51] for by acting as the spokesperson for the women in flight, she is the detector of evil and the recorder of the magical, unthinkable events taking place.

Nagatani uses children in the same way, not only to symbolize a higher consciousness, which the artist shares, but at the same time to stand for the ultimate in human vulnerability. The photographer's son, Methuen, provides him with a vantage point that infiltrates the imagery throughout the series. In *Radon Gas* (Plate 34), Met's first-grade classroom at the Monte Vista Elementary School is decorated with a chart plotting the ephemeral and yet enduring life cycle of the butterfly. Green radon gas permeates the space as the teacher, whose form appears to be overcome by the green, addresses the class from behind a gas mask. The children remain oblivious to the threat by retaining their "true colors."

In *Radium Springs* (Plate 30) Met isn't so lucky. Out with his parents on a summer's day, he's been swimming in "radium springs," a lurid green pool that Nagatani has invented in the distance. It has left its mark on the child's little torso, which is a deathly shade of grey green up to his armpits. Nonetheless, he welcomes us to this gradually metamorphosing landscape, and we soon notice that his father and mother have joined the radium community in also wearing the green shadow on their bodies.

In playful allusion to the code names for the first combat atomic bomb that looked like "an elongated trash can with fins,"[52] Met turns up as "Little Boy" (the uranium gun) holding a toy airplane at Cannon Air Force Base next to a Polaroid SX-70 image of a "Fat Man" (the implosion bomb) held skyward by a disembodied black-gloved hand watching a display of F-111D's in the 27th Tactical Fighter Wing (Plate 22). Thus Nagatani's boy is a symbolic extension of himself. Everywhere that Met appears Nagatani stages him as the supreme lover of toys, games, excursions, and mechanical experiments, capable of being absorbed into the fanciful web of warfare, weaponry, and military superiority.[53] The child drinks it all in, able to revel in such signs and symbols which proclaim the Cannon base "1988 Air Force Winner, Commander-in-Chief's Installation Excellence Award."

Children appear in two of Nagatani's most textbook-like images, which, like the

Plate 34

Plate 30

High Street picture (Plate 31), draw an insidious power from the banality of the architecture and soulless color and design. In *Missile Display, Robert Goddard High School, New Mexico,* 1990 (Plate 29) young people in Roswell, New Mexico, confront us like ghosts. They are not innocent and hopeful advertisements for their alma mater, named after the father of rocketry; rather they appear as broken survivors beseeching us with hollow, accusing stares.[54] To stress the point Nagatani pasted the flags at half-mast on the flagpole and added a third missile to the two at the entrance by mounting it onto the location of a defunct "missile fountain."

Plate 29

Children make a similar appearance at the Bradbury Science Museum at Los Alamos (Plate 12) where all is arranged so that the viewer feels "very little sense of danger or dread." The military rhetoric broadcast throughout the museum consists of calculated psychic numbing.[55] In the foreground Nagatani places the statement of Donald M. Kerr, director of Los Alamos Laboratory from 1979 to 1985. Acting like a credo it appears next to a color photograph of an exploding bomb:

If peace is viewed as the absence of general war among the major states, the world has enjoyed more years of peace since 1945 than has been known in this century, and nuclear weapons have been a major force working for peace in the postwar world. They make the cost of war seem frighteningly high and thus discourage nations from starting wars that might lead to their use.

Plate 12

In this context all Nagatani can think of is the Peace Museum at Hiroshima where sealed flasks of charred human body parts are displayed, partly to document, partly to shock. He is inspired by early scenes in *Hiroshima Mon Amour* that show photographs of the victims exhibited in the museum. He asks the Chemistry Department at the University of New Mexico for a donation of flasks and receives them with no questions asked. He fills the flasks with pale grey wood ash from a friend's fireplace.

When his nieces and nephew visit from Los Angeles he lures them into playing with grey makeup that he's bought from Disco Display in Albuquerque. This is how he drains the color from the faces of Ayame, Alyssa, and Brett Nagatani, his brother's children. They are the phantoms of lost souls which surface among the names that the photographer's mother has written in simplified Japanese characters on the papers in the flasks.

According to the photograph, museums are places where adults take children to learn things. The insidious simplicity of this allows Nagatani to make much of the doubled-edged symbolism in static missile displays, the missile parks, and the atomic "science" museum, where American National Defense publicly goes on the defensive, especially as this might be experienced by children. In such places the obvious annihilating power of the weapons is subsumed in absurdly contradictory arguments and declarations of peace, for our current experience reveals clearly that the "frighteningly high" cost of weapons does *not* "discourage nations from starting wars that might lead to their use."

When Nagatani's son, Met, and his cub scout buddy visit the H+ Injector, LAMPF Accelerator in the physics "facility" at Los Alamos (Plate 13), they are good, little American citizens following the rules, and they seem to obey as they watch a couple of regular-looking civilians with long poles performing "a strange scientific function" with hydrogen ions that might as well be some sort of fishing, for the lustrous walls aquatically gleam and shimmer. "No Hunting without Permission," says the sign; but someone's caught a turtle on a rope knotted the way a kid might do it. The animal dangles on this leash in front of the window leading to the accelerator as if looking for his home in an aquarium. As with other symbolic animals which dramatize the meaning of many compositions in the series (milking cow, rabbit, sheep, roadrunner, bat, golden eagle, and carp) Nagatani ascribes to the turtle mythical powers which Japanese artists in the nineteenth century associated with animals.

Plate 13

Nagatani has the eagle, carp, and turtle repeat the symbolic functions they served in the wood-block prints of Hiroshige. Turtles, eels, and carp were bred in Japan to be sold, but there was a custom in which they were released into rivers near well-traveled bridges in a Buddhist ritual called hōjō-e, the "releasing of life," which built up positive karma and expressed the Buddhist prohibition against killing living things.[56] Thus the children drink in the scene at the facility as the turtle waits in front of the rivet-trimmed window to be released.

Following an ancient Chinese custom, in Japan on the fifth day of the fifth month little boys of six or seven are celebrated with banners depicting carp as a symbolic part of Japanese children's day, a celebration of life. To his view of the cemetery at the Laguna Pueblo Reservation (Plate 7) Nagatani adds the carp as another of the animal symbols that are so important to him. Also this is another instance in the series in which by focusing on children the photographer is able to express his own most profound fears. Again, he lifts the motif directly from a wood-block print by Hiroshige and virtually decals it to a distant view of the pueblo.[57] Through this out-of-scale graphic we gradually notice the unremarkable vista which unfolds in the space beyond, with little houses and slender telephone poles interrupted in the cemetery by clusters of white crosses, newly dug mounds of earth, and traces of plastic flowers.

Plate 7

Nagatani repeats the carp two times in this photograph, making a kind of "Trinity" of good luck; the fish also stands for Christ and the Resurrection. The poles holding the banners blend in with the telephone poles; thus through the diminishing carp, the celebration of life and renewal would also seem to diminish. The issue is especially delicate at Laguna since the inhabitants continue to live in the village of Paguate with the full knowledge that it is contaminated.

The photographer has discovered an essay in which Laguna poet Leslie Marmon Silko explains that among Native Americans all things are equal, no person is better than any other, that sacred lands may occur anywhere and that "destruction of any part of the Earth does immediate harm to all living things."[58] In the 1940s and 1950s the Jackpile uranium mine blew the earth around Laguna wide open, swallowed the entire eastern and southern parts of the village, and destroyed sacred places by digging its shafts directly under the old village with its apricot and apple orchards and fields of corn, beans, and melons. Now masses of tailings remain no more than two hundred feet from the village's present site.

On Nagatani's first visit to Laguna, the wind was strong, and he watched some boys playing basketball "in the midst of all this stuff blowing up. . . . I didn't want to stay there because that's all hot dust from the tailing deposits." He felt the dust settle on his shoulder like a great cape, and quickly after making his pictures he jumped in the car and drove away. As he explained it:

The village of Paguate in the Laguna pueblo is very dangerous. . . . Like Grants all of these places are scheduled for Superfund cleanups by the EPA. The Native Americans are victims and victimizers. They gained a lot of money for this mining. They got the money to clean up their lands; they're in charge now, and they're thriving on the cleanup funds; but they're slow.

In the series Nagatani freely blends the experiences of children with ancient Chinese, Japanese, and Native American symbols. The carp, the children's day, and the pueblo site combine easily with scenes extolling nuclear weaponry in Nagatani's general mockery. Thus it is with perfect aplomb that Nagatani depicts Kwahu, the Hopi eagle kachina levitating amid a pathetically aspiring group of missiles at the White Sands Missile Park in a gesture of power that seems pointless against the competition (Plate 24), or positions there a group of Koshare, or Tewa ritual clowns which he borrowed from the Frontier Restaurant in Albuquerque. With their convict-striped clothing and papier-mâché "horns," the Koshare look like a mixture of park guards, court jesters, and priests (Plate 25). Through photographing, cutting, mounting, and arranging, Nagatani has them dancing on the missile range, their gestures seeming to bless a sacred site, their costumes vying with the missiles that cut into the yellow heavens. We have to look closely for Nagatani's signature in this image, but there it is, dead center, in the sign which reads: "Personal Photography Permitted."

Plate 24

The sacrifice of Native American land, if not a dominant theme in *Nuclear Enchantment,* is significant in Nagatani's art of lamentation. The most dreadful of these images is perhaps that of Kweo, the wolf kachina, fierce fighter hovering over a poisoned river landscape that the United Nuclear Corporation created from 1979 to 1982 by spilling radioactive waste into the North Fork of the Rio Puerco near Gallup (Plate 9). When the photographer attended the EPA hearings he learned that this river carries water that has ten to one hundred times the maximum allowable levels of radioactivity through communities that line Interstate 40 in western New Mexico and eastern Arizona. What can supernatural powers do against such things? Kweo can only gaze into space, angry mouth agape, rattles quieted in the face of tragic destruction.

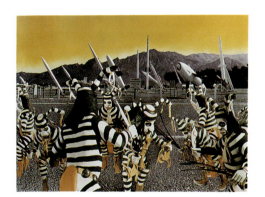

Plate 25

As with the roadrunners sacrificed at the nuclear crossroads in Vaughn

(Plate 37), sheep lie bloated and dead in the river. They were sent there by the Navajo, not only because there is no other place for them to drink, but because the residents still do not comprehend the extent of the danger. As Raymond Morgan, the community liaison for the Puerco River Education Project, observed, "Explaining uranium and its effects to traditional Navajos is like trying to explain a light bulb to someone who has been blind all their life."

To convey his own disbelief Nagatani pastes a photograph of the wolf kachina to another photograph of the river. Then for the corpses he photographs toy sheep which he cuts out and pastes onto the river shot. Horrible little bodies they are but, in fact, they are benign symbols against reports that a butchered sheep in the Lupton area that had to be taken away and buried because it smelled so bad after drinking from the water.[59] "Studies say that it's just about OK to drink, which means not to touch it. It's still not as bad as downtown Los Angeles water," Nagatani muses.[60]

Plate 35

Who among the Native Americans is not "blind," according to Nagatani? Again, conscience seems to lie with the children. The only person watching the story of WIPP site nuclear waste on the evening news (Plate 35) in a Native American dwelling is a young boy. The rest of the family, dressed for a festival, is absorbed in distancing itself from the issues by relegating them to abstractions, all interrelated, and building one upon the other in a Scrabble game consisting of words such as LIFE, PILING, GNOME, SHEEP, LAGUNA, RADIOACTIVE, NAGASAKI, ATOMIC, BOMB, RED, and not insignificantly, HERO.

Plate 38

What causes heroic cultures to die? Nagatani asks. He goes to Chaco Canyon and meditates on the splendid ruins of Pueblo Bonito. He considers the mystery surrounding the sudden disappearance of the Anasazi peoples. What devastated their economy? And what would happen to New Mexico if all weapons development were halted, if the nuclear industry folded? "If Atomic Economy Shrinks, What Next?" says the clipping held by the woman as she approaches "the great ruins of an ancient Indian fortified town" (Plate 38), to which scene Nagatani positions an F-117A Stealth fighter about to disappear into a perfectly placed mushroom-like cloud.[61]

38

BRILLIANT PEBBLES AND A PARABLE

"Declassified into dust, all species, no matter large or small, are continuously being measured for extinction."[62] Didn't the disappearance of the dinosaurs lead to great deposits of fuel in the earth? What a grand sacrifice from which we can only benefit. The land is a great repository of all that has passed, a great sacrificial altar with all things upon it in the slow or sudden process of transformation. Nagatani brings the dinosaurs back for another endurance test; he has them infiltrate a contamination area at Sandia National Laboratories (Plate 15). They are not happy at this site. Their mouths open to show teeth that have nothing to chew; they gasp for air. What will their radioactive bodies produce for future fuels?

Plate 15

When Nagatani goes to the Nuclear Engineering Building at the University of New Mexico to find the Aerojet General Nucleonics Reactor (AGN-201 M112) he discovers evidence of serious change in a revolt of "transformers." Militant red and blue plastic Gobots are attacking the lab (Plate 32), while a flank of metal transformers occupies the top of the file cabinet, and Teenage Mutant Ninja Turtles, newly hatched from some radioactive sewer, wrangle in the next room. The humans are gone, the traces of their pathetic ingenuity consisting of a table full of mousetraps with which some physicist used to demonstrate to students a nuclear chain reaction.

Plate 32

The nuclear world is so magical why not show the excitement of its positive splendors? But the photographer discovers when he is at the Sandia National Laboratories that he is incapable of making an image of the Particle Beam Fusion Accelerator II with its 100 trillion watts of pulsing energy, which join together the nuclei of light atoms in fusion, the fuel for which exists in hydrogen in water in virtually inexhaustible quantities. He stands on the bridge with his camera, loving the magenta electrical flashovers in the magnetic fields and the blue electrical arcs showing the electrical energy switched for pulse-forming produced during a shot. But he can't make the picture look like what he sees. So he gets permission to use one issued by the laboratory as a publicity shot. He discovers that it is a picture that won a prize.

He makes this prize-winning vision of swirling magenta and blue lights the central focus for *Magic/Myth/Megaton* (Plate 14), for its effect is magically disorienting. He gives a student named Sarah twenty-five dollars to rent evening clothes from Mr. Tux in order to look like a magician. He finds a top hat for five dollars in a thrift shop. Then he lures Coconut, a white rabbit, away from a friend of his son's. In the studio the creature sits in a cage eating carrots and sucking on a piece of string.

Plate 14

The photographer wants the magician to pull the rabbit from a black top hat on command in a gesture of bravura while he positions an image of an Australian aborigine opposite the image of the Particle Beam Fusion Accelerator. After taking an hour to adjust the lighting to make two black-and-white Polaroid tests, which determine an exposure of four seconds at an f-stop of $45^1/_3$, they are ready for the rabbit. Coconut is frightened by all the people there for the shot and by the lights (each has a 1,000-watt bulb, which is hardly comparable to the wattage of the Particle Beam Fusion Accelerator, after all). The rabbit keeps its nose down in the hat while the assistants whistle to try and coax it out. After all of this squirming, white hairs cover the hat and have to be removed with masking tape, for the photographer wants the shot to be impeccably dark and glossy. Coconut ends up cradled in the hat like a hen warming its eggs, while the magician raises a gloved hand over its head, protectively, as if blessing the creature. The result has nothing to do with what the photographer originally wanted; yet he decides that its complete serenity is perfect.

At the end of the day the photographer and his son go to look at the city lights of Albuquerque's downtown. The boy wears a hat with a brim, a miniature of his father's. It has started to rain, and the father raises a protective umbrella. Holding hands they gaze into the distance at two extinct volcanos. The city doesn't have pretty lights. These are subsumed in the red glow of the setting sun and a thick overhanging cloud which shrouds the sunset and threatens to absorb the pair.[63] Rain starts to fall in stinging, black torrents, but the man and the child stand firm and contented in each other's company, oblivious to any danger. Neither sees the "space trash" overhead. They don't realize the secret "Star Wars" being fought by thousands of "Brilliant Pebbles," each housed in its own solar-powered cocoon,

40

circling the earth at 11,000 mph, with electronic eyes ("Popeye" star trackers, and "Seekers") intercepting enemy launch missiles.[64] The pair doesn't see the satellites for cable television or long-distance telephone calls that burn out after several revolutions of the earth, like the brief cycle of the butterfly. Nagatani has carefully arranged these bits of brilliance overhead so that they will be ignored by the man and his son, for in this final image the photographer has decided to favor something sweeter.

There is a parable, much repeated by students of Zen, about a man traveling across a field who encountered a tiger:

He fled, the tiger after him. Coming to a precipice, he caught hold of the root of a wild vine and swung himself over the edge. The tiger sniffed at him from above. Trembling, the man looked down to where from below, another tiger was waiting to eat him. Only the vine sustained him. Two mice, one white, one black, little by little started to gnaw away the vine. The man saw a luscious strawberry near him. Grasping the vine with one hand, he plucked the strawberry with the other. How sweet it tasted![65]

Plate 40

The Japanese-American photographer holds the traditional umbrella for protection from the elements, but with his other hand he grasps the sweet fruit in the figure of the child, his son, but also the child who represents the very soul of the artist himself, and that which makes his art possible. As an artist facing a nuclear world Nagatani absorbed its ominous beauty. Like the Particle Beam Fusion Accelerator, he became a great receiving pool, reflector of the high-energy fields bouncing off the field of his own imagination. But if he shows genius as an artist it is as *homo ludens,* a man forever at play. He knows, like the wisest of children's writers, if asked what the difference is between death and strawberries, that "we care more about strawberries."[66] And that between fate and love, "there is no difference."

NOTES

1. Originally Nagatani envisioned the project as a photographic/literary collaboration with Joel Weishaus, a poet living in Albuquerque, New Mexico, who has been conducting

his own investigations into the state's nuclear dream. Weishaus has written elaborate commentaries which explore in some depth the mythical thinking suggested by each of Nagatani's nuclear images. His notes to the commentaries, which meander through sources that range widely in nuclear literature, anthropology, ethnography, symbolist poetry, folk art, the history of the saints, weaponry, and dinosaurs, to suggest a few, are more detailed than his initial text, a practice that suggests a conscious allusion to the hair-splitting of religious exegesis. Thus, this writing, at once passionate, self-consciously archival, and rich in obscure personal associations, seems to affect a literary mode more common among the fathers of the Catholic church or of talmudic scholars and expresses the pluralism associated with much other art in the late twentieth century. Collected under the title of *The Deeds and Sufferings of Light,* it accompanied the exhibition of *Nuclear Enchantment.*

2. Principally, these people include photographer Anthony Richardson; color photographer and color printer Scott Vlaun; and Diane Keane, a painter and photographer who produced many of the backdrops in the studio where the large installations were constructed. Nagatani lists the names of many others and clarifies their roles in the work in the Acknowledgments.

3. See "Fukagawa Susaki Jūmantsubo," in *Hiroshige, 100 Famous Views of Edo,* exhibition catalogue, preface by Robert Buck, introductory essays by Henry D. Smith II, and Amy G. Poster; plate commentaries by Henry D. Smith (Brooklyn and New York: Brooklyn Museum and George Braziller, 1986), plate 107.

4. Jonathan Schell, *The Fate of the Earth* (New York: Alfred Knopf, 1982), p. 12.

5. Patrick Nagatani, from taped conversations with the author from June through December of 1990. In the present essay all direct quotations from the photographer derive from these conversations and will not be further credited in any subsequent citations.

6. The photographer quotes this from William M. Arkin and Richard W. Fieldhouse, *Nuclear Battlefields* (Cambridge, Mass.: Ballinger Publishing Co., 1985) in several proposals requesting funding for this project.

7. Lansing Lamont, *Day of Trinity* (New York: Atheneum, 1985), p. x.

8. Ibid., p. 12.

9. Richard Rhodes, *The Making of the Atomic Bomb* (New York: Simon and Schuster, 1986), p. 657.

10. Ibid., p. 668.

11. Schell, *The Fate of the Earth,* p. 150.

12. Ibid., p. 151.

13. Spencer R. Weart, *Nuclear Fear: A History of Images* (Cambridge, Mass.: Harvard University Press, 1988), pp. 413, 421–26.

14. This refers to a group of photographers now confronting "the human conquest of

nature" by heavy industry in *The New American Pastoral Landscape Photography in the Age of Questioning,* an exhibition organized by the International Museum of Photography at George Eastman House, Rochester, New York, catalogue essay by Robert Sobieszek, 1990. It traveled to the Whitney Museum of American Art at Equitable Center, New York, July 11–September 8, 1990.

15. The plaque reads as follows: PROJECT GASBUSSY, NUCLEAR EXPLOSIVE EMPLACEMENT/REENTRY WELL [GB-ER] SITE OF THE FIRST UNITED STATES UNDERGROUND NUCLEAR EXPERIMENT FOR THE STIMULATION OF LOW-PRODUCTIVITY GAS RESERVOIRS. A 29-KILOTON NUCLEAR EXPLOSIVE WAS DETONATED AT A DEPTH OF 4227 FEET BELOW THIS SURFACE LOCATION ON DECEMBER 10, 1967.

NO EXCAVATION, DRILLING, AND/OR REMOVAL OF MATERIALS TO A TRUE VERTICAL DEPTH OF 1500 FEET IS PERMITTED WITHIN A RADIUS OF 100 FEET OF THIS SURFACE LOCATION. NOR ANY SIMILAR EXCAVATION, DRILLING, AND/OR REMOVAL OF SUBSURFACE MATERIALS BETWEEN THE TRUE VERTICAL DEPTHS OF 1500 FEET AND 4500 FEET IS PERMITTED WITHIN A 600 FOOT RADIUS OF T 29 N. R 4 W. NEW MEXICO PRINCIPAL MERIDIAN, RIO ARRIBA COUNTY, NEW MEXICO, WITHOUT U.S. GOVERNMENT PERMISSION. UNITED STATES DEPARTMENT OF ENERGY, NOVEMBER, 1978.

16. Nagatani originally wanted an effect of thousands of cockroaches in the foreground and still possesses a notebook of cockroach shots that he made in the University of New Mexico Biology Department. He gave up the idea in favor of photographer Betty Hahn's blue hands and the fake rubber bugs in her collection that simply looked better when photographed. Each of the forty images in the present publication has come into being with a similar background of many trials, false starts, and retrials leading circuitously and suggestively to success in the final result.

17. "On Location," and "Editorial," *Defense World* (June/July 1989), pp. 5, 1.

18. In "Nuclear Disarmament as a Moral Certainty," in *Nuclear Deterrence, Ethics and Strategy,* eds. Russell Hardin, John J. Mearsheimer, Gerald Dworkin, and Robert Goodin (Chicago and London: University of Chicago Press, 1985), p. 269.

19. Schell, *The Fate of the Earth,* p. 209.

20. Ibid., p. 62.

21. Published in 1980 by the American Nuclear Society, which also distributed "Nuclear Energy Facts, Questions and Answers."

22. Schell, *The Fate of the Earth,* p. 53.

23. David Morrissey, "Drugs Linked to 14 Arrests of Base Elite," *Albuquerque Journal* (March 1, 1987), pp. A1, A8.

24. Lawrence Spohn, "The Trestle," *Albuquerque Tribune* (May 8, 1989), p. C1.

25. Nagatani achieved the image on the TV not with collage, which would have been so simple, but entirely with electronic technologies. He focused a high-end video camera on

Del Tredici's 8-×-10-inch picture which was mounted near the sink outside of the boundaries of the still life and transferred the image to the television monitor.

26. Actually, the glow is the result of red gels that the photographer applied to the outside of the kitchen windows.

27. Another such "table of contents" which shows off his passion for missile and model plane building occurs in *A7-D, 150th TAC Fighter Group, New Mexico Air National Guard, Kirtland Air Force Base, Albuquerque, New Mexico* (Plate 16), which displays the weapons around the airplane as neatly as a proud shopkeeper might dress a window.

28. Associated Press, "Chemical Blast Rocks Desert of New Mexico," *Albuquerque Journal* (June 2, 1989), p. D4.

29. Robert Chadwell Williams, *Klaus Fuchs, Atom Spy* (Cambridge, Mass.: Harvard University Press, 1987), passim.

30. Williams illustrates in chart form the hierarchical network of names of spies, couriers, etc. from 1945 until the middle 1950s. Ibid., p. 71.

31. Clinton P. Anderson, with Milton Viorst, *Outsider in the Senate* (New York and Cleveland: World Publishing Company, 1970), p. 172.

32. In the late summer 1986 Morrissey published several articles on the accident for the *Albuquerque Journal,* based on government documents. I quote from Nagatani's clippings of some of these, "H-Bomb Impact Site 'Cold'" (September 6, 1986), pp. A1, A3 which describes the incident and gives the vital statistics and "Witness Recalls Blast, Disputes 'Turbulence'" (September 6, 1986), p. A3, which quotes "Pete" Gardner, pilot of the small plane. See also David H. Morrissey, "Documents Explain Kirtland Accident," *Albuquerque Journal* (August 27, 1986), pp. A1, A3.

33. Schell, *The Fate of the Earth,* p. 78.

34. David H. Morrissey, "First Volume on Sandia History Completed," *Albuquerque Journal* (March 22, 1989), p. D1. This book by Necah S. Furman called *Sandia National Laboratories, The Postwar Decade* was published in Albuquerque by the University of New Mexico Press in 1989. It has 750 pages.

35. Byron Spice, "Air Force to Build Telescope in Manzanos," *Albuquerque Journal* (March 28, 1989), pp. A1, A3.

36. This article, clipped from the *Albuquerque Journal* or the *Tribune* sometime between 1987 and 1990, is among many in the photographer's veritable *millefeuille* of research papers for which it has been virtually impossible to ascertain a precise date.

37. Karl F. Moffatt, "Huge Yucca Found at WSMR Sets Record," *Albuquerque Journal* (June 25, 1989), p. D2.

38. C. V. Glines, "The Bat Bombers," *Air Force Magazine* (October 1990), pp. 88–91.

39. Charles Berlitz and William L. Moore, *The Roswell Incident* (New York: Grosset and Dunlap, 1980). The story is even more fantastic than Nagatani recollects. The debris of the

crash on a ranch near Roswell contained "a large flying saucer and the remains of half a dozen or so humanoid creatures, pale in skin coloring, about four feet tall, and dressed in a kind of one piece jumpsuit uniform." Plus there was "a great quantity of highly unusual wreckage, much of it metallic in nature, apparently originating from the same object." It was described as "nothing made on earth." There were also "columns of hieroglyphic-like writing . . . on a wooden-like substance (that was not wood) and similar unknown lettering on the control panels of the disc or saucer" (pp. 27–28). The heads of the occupants were "larger in proportion to their bodies" (p. 55). Their eyes were "small and oddly spaced" (p. 57). Other occupants found in another desert area related to the Roswell crash (one of which was alive when found) had throats "badly burned" from inhaling the fumes which made it impossible for them to talk. Several were "taken to California and kept alive in respirators" (p. 82). A full description of the aliens with drawings of their skinny bodies and delicately webbed hands appears on pp. 92–103.

40. United States Environmental Protection Agency, *Quarterly Status Report of Superfund Sites* 1, no. 3 (July 1988), p. 3. See also from the same agency, Office of Waste Programs Enforcement, *Environmental Fact Sheet, The Superfund Enforcement Process: How It Works* (Spring 1988).

41. "Yotsuya Naitō Shinjuku" in *Hiroshige, 100 Famous Views of Edo* (1857) shows the horse. Nagatani found it humorous and wanted a similar effect. First he had Jeffrey Sippel, a printmaker, draw the cow pie, but he ended up using the painter Michael Cook's more simplified drawing instead.

42. Jean-Pierre Cativiela, "Church Rock clean up, United Nuclear 'ready, anxious' for mine mill job," source unknown, from the photographer's files, which also included two other clippings: "Uranium cleanup plan outlined by UNC," and "EPA sets mine open house."

43. Prepared by the Waste Management Technology at Sandia National Laboratories for the U.S. Department of Energy, Waste Isolation Pilot Plant, Carlsbad, New Mexico, p. 3.

44. Weart, *Nuclear Fear,* p. 298.

45. "'Low Level' Description Doesn't Mean Harmless," *Albuquerque Journal* (May 21, 1989), p. A8. See also Chuck McCutcheon, "WIPP Debate Goes Beyond N.M.," *Albuquerque Journal* (May 21, 1989), pp. A1 and A8, and Chuck McCutcheon, "Objections Mar Road to WIPP," *Albuquerque Journal* (April 8, 1990), pp. C1 and C2.

46. Fritz Thompson, "Nuclear Age Puts Vaughn at Crossroads," *Albuquerque Journal* (September 25, 1988), p. C1.

47. The largest studio was a gutted floor over Ray Graham's gallery "Cafe" in Albuquerque. Here Nagatani installed the compositions essentially conceived and rendered in the manner in which he had photographed with the Polaroid 20- × -24 view

camera, where live figures or cardboard cutouts of human figures against backgrounds, hand colored or color photographed, dominated a scene. The images worked in this way form a sort of transitional group leading to the *Enchantment* series and ultimately appear throughout it as: *Trinitite, Ground Zero, Trinity Site, New Mexico,* 1988–89 (Plate 1); *Trinity Site, Jornada del Muerto, New Mexico,* 1989 (Plate 2); *Nike-Hercules Missile Monument, St. Augustine Pass, Highway 70, White Sands Missile Range, New Mexico,* 1989 (Plate 26); *"Lysistratus," National Atomic Museum, Albuquerque, New Mexico,* 1989 (Plate 19), and *National Atomic Museum, Kirtland Air Force Base, Albuquerque, New Mexico,* 1989 (Plate 18). The method for producing this group of pictures is virtually the same for all of them and links the work back to Nagatani's previous style of the early and middle 1980s. As the figure numbers show, they are not necessarily arranged in the new series in a way that would suggest that they are among those made first.

48. Roland Barthes, "Food Decentered," *Empire of Signs,* trans. by Richard Howard (New York: Hill and Wang, 1982), p. 20.

49. Ibid., "Chopsticks," pp. 17–18.

50. Weart, *Nuclear Fear,* p. 367.

51. She is Martie Geiger, who, while studying sculpture and ceramics at the University of New Mexico, worked as a nurse at a M.A.S.H. unit in the army. She appears in a similar gesture in *"Fin de Siècle," Bat Flight Amphitheater, Carlsbad Caverns, New Mexico,* 1989 (Plate 39).

52. Rhodes, *The Making of the Atom Bomb,* p. 701. It was ten and a half feet long and twenty-nine inches in diameter and weighed 9,700 pounds.

53. Some thirteen of the forty images in *Nuclear Enchantment* use children as principal message carriers for Nagatani's symbolism. This is true for over half the images if we add to this number the images that include airplane models, children's toys, or pets.

54. The young people in this composition are actually photography students from Loyola Marymount University in Los Angeles whose faces are documented in Nagatani's vast negative bank, which includes portraits of most of the people he has taught. Among those from Loyola Marymount he had ninety possibilities to choose from. Although the students were "wholesome and middle class" he looked for faces that were "vacant and hollow." He mounted blow-ups of their figures onto foam core board and during the exposure allowed the camera to record them for only a few seconds. Then he flipped this board down, as if on a hinge, and continued to finish the exposure, in order that the figures would read like phantoms.

55. Nagatani was inspired to do the shot of the Bradbury Science Museum at Los Alamos National Laboratory by Peter N. Kirstein's article, "The Atomic Museum," in *Art in America* (June 1989), pp. 45–57, where the author discusses Bradbury in terms of psychic denial that stresses the "friendly," "fun," and "useful" effects of atomic arsenals.

56. See "Fukagawa Mannenbashi," commentary by Henry D. Smith II in *Hiroshige, 100 Famous Views of Edo,* Plate 56.

57. In "Suidōbashi Surugadai," from *Hiroshige, 100 Famous Views of Edo,* Plate 48.

58. "The Fourth World," *ArtForum,* reprinted with permission of the author and ArtForum International in *Playing with Fire: Six New Mexico Artists Working with Nuclear Issues,* exhibition catalogue, Santa Fe, Center for Contemporary Arts, November 9–December 22, 1990.

59. Richard Sitts, "Houck warned of Puerco," newspaper clipping from the photographer's files.

60. Nagatani endured living in a downtown Los Angeles loft from 1981 through 1984, surviving the dust, poor water, and buildings made fragile through earthquakes.

61. The photographer explains that the placement of the cloud was no accident; nor was it the result of cutting and pasting but of simply waiting until it positioned itself neatly over the ruins.

62. Joel Weishaus, "Sandia Dinosaurs," see note 1.

63. This image, like many in the series, achieves its startling effects through superior printing. In the negative, the sky was not as dark or ominous as it appears in the final result, nor was the effect of the sunset so intense. With Scott Vlaun, a master color printer who punched up the color, Nagatani evolved and sustained his ideas through an elaborate creative process that continues to be refined long after the shot was conceived and staged into every phase of realizing the work. The approach distinguishes Nagatani's recent working methods by being more refined than ever before. Nagatani and Vlaun's conversations in the darkroom (recorded by this writer in the summer of 1990) have the quality of an intense musical rehearsal with the players rewriting their instrumentation as they go.

64. Dan Stober, "Brilliant Pebbles Savior or Hot Air?" *Albuquerque Journal* (May 20, 1990), pp. B1–B4. See also Dan Stober, "Critics Say 'Pebbles' System Faces Rocky Road to Success," *Albuquerque Journal* (May 20, 1990), p. B1.

65. "A Parable," in "101 Zen Stories," *Zen Flesh, Zen Bones: A Collection of Zen and Pre-Zen Writings,* compiled by Paul Reps (Rutland, Vermont, and Tokyo, Japan: Charles E. Tuttle Co., 1957), pp. 38–39.

66. Cooper Edens. See his *Now Is the Moon's Eyebrow* (San Diego: Green Tiger Press, 1987), passim.

THE PLATES

1. Trinitite, Ground Zero, Trinity Site, New Mexico, 1988–89 (collaborated in part with Andrée Tracey).

2. Trinity Site, Jornada del Muerto, New Mexico, 1989.

3. Ground Zero, "Operation Gnome" (December 10, 1961), 48 Kilometers Southeast of Carlsbad, New Mexico, 1990 (collaborated in part with Shereen Lobdell).

4. Plaque, Ground Zero, "Project Gasbuggy" (December 10, 1967), Carson National Forest, New Mexico, 1990.

5. "Cow Pie/Yellow Cake," Uranium Mine, Homestake Mining Company, near Mt. Taylor, Milan, and Grants, New Mexico, 1989.

6. Uranium Tailings, Anaconda Minerals Corporation, Laguna Pueblo Reservation, New Mexico, 1990.

7. Japanese Children's Day Carp Banners, Paguate Village, Jackpile Mine Uranium Tailings, Laguna Pueblo Reservation, New Mexico, 1990.

8. Golden Eagle, United Nuclear Corporation Uranium Mill and Tailings,
   Church Rock, New Mexico, 1990.

9. Kweo/Wolf Kachina, United Nuclear Corporation Uranium Tailings Spill,
    North Fork of Rio Puerco, near Gallup, New Mexico, 1989.

10. "Bida Hi"/Opposite Views, Northeast—Navajo Tract Homes and Uranium
    Tailings, Southwest—Shiprock, New Mexico, 1990.

11. Contaminated Radioactive Sediment, Mortandad Canyon, Los Alamos
    National Laboratory, New Mexico, 1990.

12. "Effects of Nuclear Weapons," Bradbury Science Museum, Los Alamos National Laboratory, New Mexico, 1990.

13. *"Hōjō-e*/Releasing of Life," H_+ Injector, LAMPF Accelerator, Clinton P. Anderson Meson Physics Facility, Los Alamos National Laboratory, New Mexico, 1991.

14. Magic/Myth/Megaton, Particle Beam Fusion Accelerator II, Sandia
    National Laboratories, Albuquerque, New Mexico, 1990.

15. Contamination Area, Building #3, Sandia National Laboratories, Kirtland
    Air Force Base, Albuquerque, New Mexico, 1989.

16. "A7-D, 150th TAC Fighter Group, New Mexico Air National Guard, Kirtland Air Force Base, Albuquerque, New Mexico, 1989.

17. "Simulation/Simulation," The Trestle, Nuclear Effects (Electromagnetic Pulses) Simulation Facility, Air Force Weapons Laboratory, Kirtland Air Force Base, Albuquerque, New Mexico, 1990.

18. National Atomic Museum, Kirtland Air Force Base, Albuquerque, New Mexico, 1989 (collaborated in part with Andrée Tracey).

19. "Lysistratus," National Atomic Museum, Albuquerque, New Mexico, 1989.

20. B-36/Mark 17 H-Bomb Accident (May 22, 1957), 5^1/$_2$ Miles South of
    Gibson Boulevard, Albuquerque, New Mexico, 1991.

21. F-16 Falcons (U.S.A.F. Thunderbird Team), Residential Backyard Facing
    Hollowed-out Manzano Mountain Nuclear Warhead Storage Area,
    Kirtland Air Force Base, Albuquerque, New Mexico, 1990.

22. "Fat Man and Little Boy," F-111D's, 27th Tactical Fighter Wing, Cannon
Air Force Base, near Clovis, New Mexico, 1990.

CANNON AFB

1988 AIR FORCE WINNER
COMMANDER-IN-CHIEF'S
INSTALLATION EXCELLENCE
AWARD

23. "Passage of Time," Unidentified Flying Objects, F-15's of the 49th TAC Fighter Wing, Holloman Air Force Base, near Alamogordo, New Mexico, 1990.

24. Kwahu/Hopi Eagle Kachina, White Sands Missile Range, New Mexico,
    1989.

25. Koshare/Tewa Ritual Clowns, Missile Park, White Sands Missile Range, New Mexico, 1989.

26. Nike-Hercules Missile Monument, St. Augustine Pass, Highway 70, White Sands Missile Range, New Mexico, 1989.

27. Alamogordo Chamber of Commerce, New Mexico, 1990.

28. Rocket Lounge, Alamogordo, New Mexico, 1989.

29. Missile Display, Robert Goddard High School, Roswell, New Mexico, 1990.

30. Radium Springs, New Mexico, 1989.

31. Gold and Greenglass 1945 "Jello Box Halves," Atomic Spies Meeting
Place, 209 High Street, Apt. 4, Albuquerque, New Mexico, 1990.

32. "Transformers," Aerojet General Nucleonics Reactor (AGN-201 M-112), Nuclear Engineering Building, University of New Mexico, Albuquerque, New Mexico, 1990.

33. Radiation Therapy Room, Albuquerque, New Mexico, 1989.

34. Radon Gas, Elementary School Classroom, Albuquerque, New Mexico, 1990.

35. The Evening News, Native American Pueblo Dwelling, New Mexico, 1990.

36. **Waste Isolation Pilot Plant TRUPACT II Accident, Atomic Auto Wreckers, near Las Cruces, New Mexico, 1990.**

37. Waste Isolation Pilot Plant Nuclear Crossroads, U.S. 285, 60, 54, Vaughn, New Mexico, 1989.

38. F-117A Stealth Fighter, Pueblo Bonito, Chaco Culture National Historical Park, New Mexico, 1990.

39. "Fin de Siècle," Bat Flight Amphitheater, Carlsbad Caverns, New Mexico, 1989.

40. "Generation to Generation," Strategic Defense Initiative (SDI) Nuclear-Powered Vehicles, West Mesa, Albuquerque, New Mexico, 1991.

LIST OF PHOTOGRAPHS

1. Trinitite, Ground Zero, Trinity Site, New Mexico, 1988–89 (collaborated in part with Andrée Tracey).
2. Trinity Site, Jornada del Muerto, New Mexico, 1989.
3. Ground Zero, "Operation Gnome" (December 10, 1961), 48 Kilometers Southeast of Carlsbad, New Mexico, 1990 (collaborated in part with Shereen Lobdell).
4. Plaque, Ground Zero, "Project Gasbuggy" (December 10, 1967), Carson National Forest, New Mexico, 1990.
5. "Cow Pie/Yellow Cake," Uranium Mine, Homestake Mining Company, near Mt. Taylor, Milan, and Grants, New Mexico, 1989.
6. Uranium Tailings, Anaconda Minerals Corporation, Laguna Pueblo Reservation, New Mexico, 1990.
7. Japanese Children's Day Carp Banners, Paguate Village, Jackpile Mine Uranium Tailings, Laguna Pueblo Reservation, New Mexico, 1990.
8. Golden Eagle, United Nuclear Corporation Uranium Mill and Tailings, Church Rock, New Mexico, 1990.
9. Kweo/Wolf Kachina, United Nuclear Corporation Uranium Tailings Spill, North Fork of Rio Puerco, near Gallup, New Mexico, 1989.
10. "Bida Hi"/Opposite Views, Northeast—Navajo Tract Homes and Uranium Tailings, Southwest—Shiprock, New Mexico, 1990.
11. Contaminated Radioactive Sediment, Mortandad Canyon, Los Alamos National Laboratory, New Mexico, 1990.
12. "Effects of Nuclear Weapons," Bradbury Science Museum, Los Alamos National Laboratory, New Mexico, 1990.
13. "Hōjō-e/Releasing of Life," H₊ Injector, LAMPF Accelerator, Clinton P. Anderson Meson Physics Facility, Los Alamos National Laboratory, New Mexico, 1991.
14. Magic/Myth/Megaton, Particle Beam Fusion Accelerator II, Sandia National Laboratories, Albuquerque, New Mexico, 1990.
15. Contamination Area, Building #3, Sandia National Laboratories, Kirtland Air Force Base, Albuquerque, New Mexico, 1989.
16. "A7-D, 150th TAC Fighter Group, New Mexico Air National Guard, Kirtland Air Force Base, Albuquerque, New Mexico, 1989.
17. "Simulation/Simulation," The Trestle, Nuclear Effects (Electromagnetic Pulses) Simulation Facility, Air Force Weapons Laboratory, Kirtland Air Force Base, Albuquerque, New Mexico, 1990.
18. National Atomic Museum, Kirtland Air Force Base, Albuquerque, New Mexico, 1989 (collaborated in part with Andrée Tracey).
19. "Lysistratus," National Atomic Museum, Albuquerque, New Mexico, 1989.
20. B-36/Mark 17 H-Bomb Accident (May 22, 1957), 5½ Miles South of Gibson Boulevard, Albuquerque, New Mexico, 1991.
21. F-16 Falcons (U.S.A.F. Thunderbird Team), Residential Backyard Facing Hollowed-out Manzano Mountain Nuclear Warhead Storage Area, Kirtland Air Force Base, Albuquerque, New Mexico, 1990.
22. "Fat Man and Little Boy," F-111D's, 27th Tactical Fighter Wing, Cannon Air Force Base, near Clovis, New Mexico, 1990.
23. "Passage of Time," Unidentified Flying Objects, F-15's of the 49th TAC Fighter Wing, Holloman Air Force Base, near Alamogordo, New Mexico, 1990.
24. Kwahu/Hopi Eagle Kachina, White Sands Missile Range, New Mexico, 1989.
25. Koshare/Tewa Ritual Clowns, Missile Park, White Sands Missile Range, New Mexico, 1989.
26. Nike-Hercules Missile Monument, St. Augustine Pass, Highway 70, White Sands Missile Range, New Mexico, 1989.
27. Alamogordo Chamber of Commerce, New Mexico, 1990.
28. Rocket Lounge, Alamogordo, New Mexico, 1989.
29. Missile Display, Robert Goddard High School, Roswell, New Mexico, 1990.
30. Radium Springs, New Mexico, 1989.
31. Gold and Greenglass 1945 "Jello Box Halves," Atomic Spies Meeting Place, 209 High Street, Apt. 4, Albuquerque, New Mexico, 1990.
32. "Transformers," Aerojet General Nucleonics Reactor (AGN-201 M-112), Nuclear Engineering Building, University of New Mexico, Albuquerque, New Mexico, 1990.
33. Radiation Therapy Room, Albuquerque, New Mexico, 1989.
34. Radon Gas, Elementary School Classroom, Albuquerque, New Mexico, 1990.
35. The Evening News, Native American Pueblo Dwelling, New Mexico, 1990.
36. Waste Isolation Pilot Plant TRUPACT II Accident, Atomic Auto Wreckers, near Las Cruces, New Mexico, 1990.
37. Waste Isolation Pilot Plant Nuclear Crossroads, U.S. 285, 60, 54, Vaughn, New Mexico, 1989.
38. F-117A Stealth Fighter, Pueblo Bonito, Chaco Culture National Historical Park, New Mexico, 1990.
39. "Fin de Siècle," Bat Flight Amphitheater, Carlsbad Caverns, New Mexico, 1989.
40. "Generation to Generation," Strategic Defense Initiative (SDI) Nuclear-Powered Vehicles, West Mesa, Albuquerque, New Mexico, 1991.

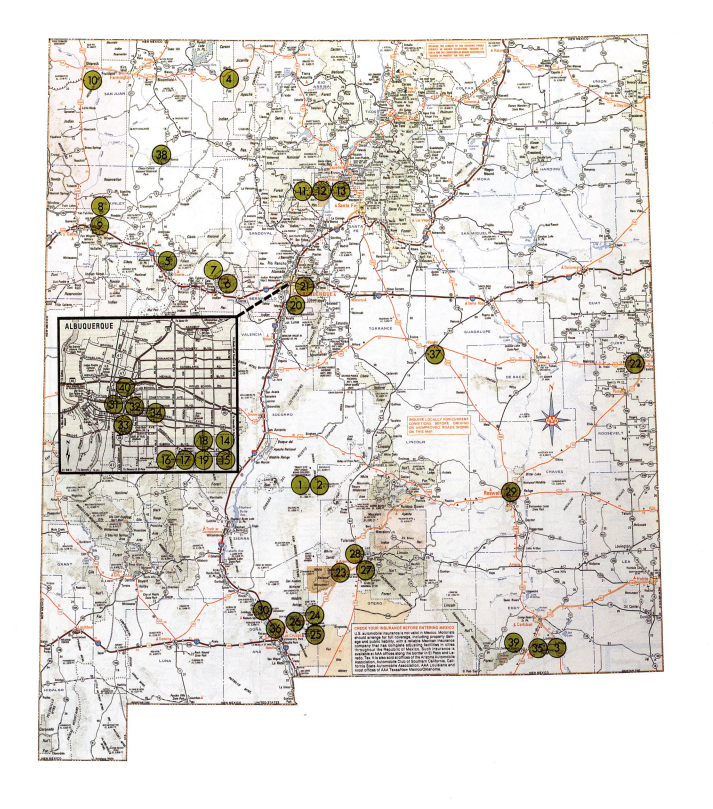

⋮⋮⋮ Minuteman II (1 warhead, 1.2-megaton yield = 100 Hiroshimas), Minuteman III (2 or 3 warheads, yield 170 to 350 kilotons each), MX (10 warheads, yield up to 300 kilotons each) ICBM silos

● Most military bases in the continental U.S. (excluding Hawaii and Alaska) including:

    air force bases
    coast guard bases
    army bases
    marine corps bases
    arsenals
    army depots
    ammunition plants
    naval air stations
    marine corps recruit depots
    naval shipyards
    weapons stations
    marine corps air stations
    military academies
    missile plants
    naval training centers
    naval ordinance stations
    submarine bases
    missile ranges
    naval weapons centers

▼ Uranium mining and milling

[C] Nuclear conversion plant

[E] Nuclear enrichment plant

[F] Nuclear fuel fabrication plant

■ Nuclear power plants (operating or under construction)

Ⓛ National laboratory (weapons development)

[MP] Material production facility (production of raw materials for a nuclear explosion)

[WP] Weapons production facility (manufacture of actual parts for the bomb)

[W] Radioactive waste depository (WIPP or Waste Isolation Pilot Plant)

◎ Trinity Site (first nuclear device successfully tested, July 16, 1945)

◎ Nevada nuclear test site

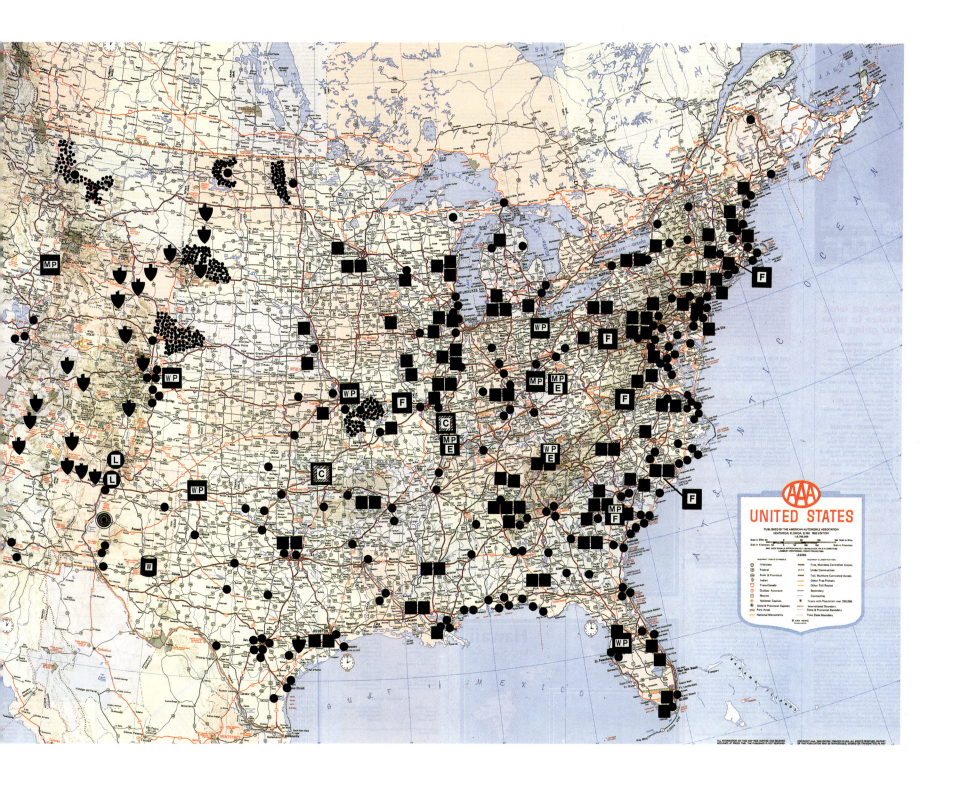

ACKNOWLEDGMENTS

After three years and countless miles traveled in New Mexico, over "j" roads and "blue highways," through small towns, air force bases, historical sites, nuclear labs, and uranium tailing deposits, I have many people to acknowledge for the production of the work and for this book.

Central are those who collaborated with me to make the work possible. Collaboration is a difficult process to establish and sustain. I have been fortunate to have had a successful six-year creative liaison with Andrée Tracey. This experience taught me the essense of what collaboration could be. The issues that we explored formed the direction for *Nuclear Enchantment.* Throughout this project, I have collaborated with Joel Weishaus. His research, information, and poetic writing resulted in his own body of literary work based on the images in this book. I am grateful for his input and support throughout this project.

Diane Keane worked as my assistant in the early pieces and expertly painted backdrops and figures of the large sets. Ray Graham allowed me to install sets in the empty space that later became his gallery Cafe in downtown Albuquerque. Anthony Richardson made many of the large-format negatives of my installations and artwork. I am particularly grateful to Scott Vlaun not only for his help with some of the setups but also for his expertise in color printing.

Others played an important role in the production of the prints. Sarah West organized and proofed the prints as they were made and gathered props and costumes, besides acting as a model. Christopher Grinnell, Ron Howard, and First Photo Corp. kept the color processor in perfect working order. Sharon Price of Ilford Corporation and Jim Sutton of Camera & Darkroom, Albuquerque, helped provide new color materials. I want to thank Carl's Darkroom/Film Processing of Albuquerque for well-processed negatives throughout the project. I am grateful to Leigh Anne Langwell, Medical Illustration and Photography, University of New Mexico, for the many copy negatives that I needed and for her modeling in early installation pictures. Paul Jeremias and Al Lopez helped print color backdrops. Shawn Driscoll, owner of Camera Graphics Photolab, Albuquerque, made many images that I used in sets or backgrounds. The work could not have been completed without Central Photographics, Chroma Color Inc., Disco Display

House, Duke City Hobbies, New Mexico Art Supply, Off Broadway, O'Malley's Glass, and Mr. Tux, all of Albuquerque.

Numerous individuals were models in the work. I thank Frank Aoi, Dan Byrne, Martie Geiger, Betty Hahn, Melvin Higashi and family, Nia Janis, Scott Kuykendall, Al Lopez, Diana G. Mehail, Kurt Mottweiller, John, Diane, Nick, Scott, Wendy, Brett, Ayame, Alyssa, and Methuen Nagatani and his dog Ziggy, Michele Naranjo, Amanda Page, Camille Pascal, Linda Rankin, Sue and Marissa Sippel, Diane Tani, Bonnie Verardo, Robert John White, Jessie Williamson, Hanna Yoshitomi, Linda Hudson and her first-grade class, and Matthew Gandart for letting me use Coconut, his rabbit. Michael Cook helped me dig craters, modeled, illustrated "cow pies," provided research information, and most of all, lent me continuous support during troubled creative times. I thank Samuel T. Bautista for his hospitality at the Laguna Pueblo Reservation and for introducing me to Loren P. Maria, Sr., and his family: Georgean, Loren Jr., Mathew, and Phyllis. I dedicate *Radiation Therapy Room, Albuquerque, New Mexico,* to the late Harry Nadler.

Special gratitude is extended to Nick Abdalla for his loan of over forty transformers from his collection. Kathryn Louise was a constant consultant. She gave me a negative for the Kirtland AFB shot and painted many background figures.

I am grateful to Robert Del Tredici, founder of the Atomic Photographer's Guild, who lent images and made me aware of nuclear issues on a global scale. Margaret Freeman offered personal anecdotes and further enlightened me on the spy saga of nuclear "secrets" in Albuquerque. She graciously allowed me to photograph in Albuquerque's original "spy" apartment with the original table on which Robert Greenglass and Harry Gold exchanged secrets. Greg MacGregor gave me a Civil Defense Geiger Counter; Skip Maisel, of Maisel's Wholesale Indian Crafts and Jewelry, loaned several Kachina dolls; Larry Rainoseck, owner of the Frontier Restaurant, lent me the Koshares that became central to an important picture in this work.

I am grateful to Ken Carpenter, electronics technician, Nuclear Engineering Lab, University of New Mexico, for access to the nuclear reactor; William L. Gannon, collections manager, Museum of Southwestern Biology, University of New Mexico, provided the birds and animals for several of the pictures; Vernard Fitzgerald gave me his old copies of *Air Force* magazine; Ken Frazer, from the Public Information Division, Sandia National Laboratories, gave me insight into the lab facilities and their function; Fred Rick, of the Public Affairs Office at Los Alamos National Laboratory, guided me on my many trips to Los Alamos; Anna Christine Hansen introduced me to theoretical physicists at Los Alamos; Lieutenant Colonel James H. Klemski, Counterintelligence Division at the U.S. Army White Sands Missile Range, provided a letter that inspired me to continue with the work and to work within the bureaucracy more diligently.

Abbas and Habiba Akhil lent me their backyard for the Manzano shot. Tarek Talet Al-Ghoussein was with me at the beginning of the project and lent me a negative for the Nike-Hercules background. Shereen Lobdell shared her sculptures in a collaborative spirit for the *Operation Gnome* image; David Morrissey, former *Albuquerque Journal* staff writer, eagerly shared information on the military sites and accidental H-bomb dropping. Michael Rosenthal loaned me video tapes and information on the Waste Isolation Pilot Plant; Jeffrey Sippel, educational director at Tamarind Institute and a native of rural Wisconsin, provided illustrations of cow pies; Arnold Venti and his family patiently put up with my search for the Gnome site on an outing to Carlsbad; and Dr. James Yamasaki, who worked with the Nagasaki children who were the victims of the atomic bomb, sensitized me to much more than the issues in New Mexico.

For providing information I thank the following institutions: U.S. Department of Energy, Albuquerque Operations Office; New Mexico Environmental Improvement Division; U.S. Environmental Protection Agency, Dallas; U.S. Department of the Interior, National Park Service, Southwestern Region, Santa Fe; Los Alamos National Laboratory, Bradbury Science Museum; Air Force Space Weapons Laboratory, Kirtland AFB, Albuquerque; Sandia National Laboratories, Public Affairs Office, Albuquerque; St. Joseph Hospital, Albuquerque; Westinghouse Electric Corporation, Waste Isolation Division, Carlsbad; and White Sands Missile Range, Public Affairs Office.

Grateful acknowledgment is made to Jim Moore and Ellen Landis of the Albuquerque Museum for exhibiting the whole project with Joel Weishaus's prose. I thank the Department of Art and Art History, the College of Fine Arts, and the Research Allocations Committee, all of the University of New Mexico.

I owe more than I can say to the staff at the University of New Mexico Press. Leading figures are Dana Asbury, art and photography editor; Elizabeth Hadas, director; and Peter Moulson, marketing director. The art director, Milenda Nan Ok Lee, designed the book and made the process creative and enjoyable.

When I first showed the work to Eugenia Parry Janis, I knew that I wanted her to write the text. Hours of taped interviews, private meetings, observation of the work in progress at all stages, and many telephone calls led to the essay. She deserves my special thanks.

Finally, I acknowledge with gratitude the contributions of my wife, Jeanean Bodwell, her parents, Herman and Peggy Bodwell, and my parents, John and Diane Nagatani. In particular, Jeanean and Methuen, my son, understand well the price paid for my commitment to this work.

Patrick Nagatani
March 1991
Albuquerque, New Mexico

NUCLEAR ENCHANTMENT

Edited by Dana Asbury
Designed by Milenda Nan Ok Lee
Typography in Helvetica
by the University of New Mexico Printing Services
Printed by Toppan Printing Co. (America), Inc.
Printed in Japan